JANELLE  18 ^{50} sw/12€

D0563859

" I am with you

always,

until the end

of time. "

(Matthew 28.20)

I AM WITH YOU

Treasured words of divine inspiration for everyone

as given to
Fr John Woolley

John Hunt
Publishing Limited

Copyright © 2001 John Hunt Publishing Ltd
Text © 1984 John Woolley

First published in Great Britain by Crown (Great Britain)
Reprinted 1985
Enlarged edition 1986 by Collins (Fount)
New edition 1991 by Crown (Great Britain)
Reprinted 1993
Reprinted 1993 by the '**I Am With You**' Foundation
New edition 1994
New edition 1996 by Arthur James Ltd.
Reprinted 1997 and 1999
Reprinted 2001, 2002 by John Hunt Publishing Ltd.

ISBN 1 85305 341 3

Write to:
John Hunt Publishing Ltd
46A West Street
Alresford
Hampshire SO24 9AU
UK

The rights of John Woolley as author of this work have been asserted
in accordance with the Copyright, Designs and Patents Act 1988.

A CIP catalogue record for this book is available from the British
Library.

Printed by Tien Wah Press Ltd, Singapore

Visit our web site at: www.johnhunt-publishing.com

I AM WITH YOU

(A new and amplified edition)

From all over the world come messages of appreciation about these words of divine encouragement and guidance from the risen Lord Jesus Christ through His Holy Spirit... words received in prayer-times by Father John Woolley, former British hospital chaplain. With the words came a promise by our Lord that there would be a wonderful spread of His word – a promise now being marvellously realised.

I Am With You offers unique help for the often-difficult Christian road, and is an essential companion for times of prayer and Bible study. These words unfailingly bring a sense of God's nearness; they bring tranquility, and they wonderfully strengthen. Church leaders, and so many readers (of all Christian denominations) speak, constantly, of being uplifted and inspired by this little book ... often in a life-changing way.

* * *

Tributes

"I commend *I Am With You* to all persons who are seeking to deepen their spiritual lives"
(Cardinal George Basil Hume, former Archbishop of Westminster, England)

"*I Am With You* is a very special book, which will bless countless people"
(Prebendary John Pearce, England)

"I have never experienced such a closeness to Jesus"
(Fran Gunning, U.S.A.)

"A lovely book of devotions; we use it daily"
(Dr Donald English, former President Methodist Conference)

"*I Am With You* will deeply touch many people"
(Robert de Grandis, U.S.A.)

"God's Holy Spirit breathes through every page"
(Revd Robert Llewelyn, England)

"The touch of God is in these beautiful words"
(Margaret Green, Canada)

"A most wonderful book which I keep with me always"
(Fr Michael Clothier, O.S.B.)

"*I Am With You* is so powerful"
(Barbara Anicich, U.S.A.)

"*I Am With You* is a little gem"
(Authoress Joyce Huggett)

"Wonderfully inspiring"   *(Betty Tapscott, U.S.A.)*

"*I Am With You* opens a lovely door into God's presence; reading it is a thing of real joy"
(Bishop John Crowley)

"Admirable for daily devotions"   *(Church Times)*

"God speaks in a very powerful way."
(Mgr Seamus Kilbane)

"I was soon head over heels in love with God's words"
(Inmate in English Prison)

"The book has changed my life"
(Fr F. Bernard, S.J., India)

"The most wonderful book I have read"
(Fr Tom Cass, Tyneside, England)

* * * *

USING THIS BOOK

Although the words in *I Am With You* are usually read in the order given in the book, there is an index at the rear for specific areas of personal need or sudden crises.

If prayer is made beforehand, so many readers have found that they turn to just the right page and that a word for the need of the moment is unfailingly given.

THE BIBLE QUOTATIONS
Bible verses – in which God speaks directly – have been chosen to accompany our Lord's words in
I Am With You.

MY PRAYER FOR YOU

+

May the Lord Jesus Christ speak to your heart, repeatedly, through His words in this book.

May He greatly bless you, and each day draw you closer to Himself.

John A. Woolley.

I am the hope of all the ends of the earth. But so few truly know it deep in their hearts. In Me lies the fulfilment of the complex desires and possibilities of human nature.

You know that all the qualities you see in Me are available for you. Are you sad, My child, that so often you fail to make use of them? Yes, this is the world's failing – that men do not appropriate that which is there for them, in Me.

Set Me before you always as your one true hope. Be sure that your hand is firmly in Mine . . . Proclaim Me as mankind's hope to those around you . . . As you recognise the progress you make with Me, so the conviction will grow which you bring to telling others, all that I can be to them!

I know that in your heart is that longing to know Me more perfectly. I honour that longing, and that is why you are sure of My patience in all your failures. It is, of course, My grace which helps you to maintain that longing – and to come, increasingly, into oneness with Myself.

I will never turn away anyone who comes to Me.

(John 6.37)

Long before My love was seen on earth it was expressed in creativity. Although seen as creativity of power or of mystery, it is a creativity of love . . . a continuing creativity.

Existence, as you see it, is puzzling and often frightening, but let it thrill you that the Father was seen in His creation ... becoming one with it, surrendering Himself to it. That moment in history when I stood as the meeting-place of Divine love and human hopes and fears, was the beginning of all true spiritual awareness.

You will be aware of much darkness, and of forces dedicated to obstructing your climb towards the heavenly sphere. Any other view of My creation would be naive and partial. Nevertheless, you must resolutely see *love* as the soul of creation... now, as it always was.

Love in creativity means that I am never remote from the inevitable heartaches of My children ... or, of course, from *your* heartaches.

Whoever has seen Me has seen the Father.

(John 14.9)

My child, let it be your privilege, each day, to dwell upon My sacrifice – made for the whole world.

In My suffering love upon the Cross you see a *continuing process* . . . the unrequited love which pursues My children – yearning for the slightest response, and profoundly grateful when one of those children surrenders his or her life to Me.

On the Cross, you see My heart of love crushed, for the moment, by the force of evil which darkens this universe. Then you see the bursting forth again of love's *power*... in My Father's victory; this power, in its submission, and its patience, can change, permanently, any human situation.

Although you are conscious of being unworthy of that love, be sure that the pain of rejection is made *so much less* by even the simplest, imperfect dependence upon Myself.

Here, at the Cross, give Me your heart, anew, every day.

**For the sake of My sheep,
I surrender My life.**

(John 10.15)

3

How much it means to Me when one of My children, responding to a prompting of My Spirit, asks to live close to Me.

The response to that request is automatic. Forces to draw closer our spirits are then at work, in spite of the tangled emotions and contra-influences of earth. As soon as that hesitant request is made, I am able to look upon My child as *perfected*.

Everything is built upon that child's request. I see beyond the intermittent progress, the spiritual weariness, and the times when that child fails Me. I need no more than the initial response, and the *continuance* of that wish to be close to Me, for My existence increasingly to inter-penetrate yours.

My child, can you still recognise that deep desire for closeness to Me in your heart . . . even after many discouragements in your spiritual walk? If so, let it remind you of the *perfection* which is your destiny.

Drawn by Me . . . with bonds of love!

(Hosea 11.4)

My child, the bond between us is unbreakable, because you are My chosen . . .

The company you keep is with the Architect of this universe in His infinite wisdom. My presence surrounds you – and My influence, in your unique circumstances. Without Me, you would have been in the gravest danger.

Because you are precious to Me, your need near to My Heart, I save you from what is contrary to your best interests, diverting harmful influences.

No combination of circumstances can defeat Me; therefore, do not be afraid of earth's chances, nor of the very worst that evil can do. Not afraid... because I can always restore and return you to the path of My will. All that you need to dwell upon is that My care of you stretches into eternity!

No-one can take My children out of My hand.
(John 10.28)

Even those who acknowledge Me carry burdens because they cannot believe that My forgiveness is *infinite;* they cannot believe that there is cleansing of the deep guilt flowing from wilful acts which had tragic consequences for others; they cannot believe that (even with true sorrow over those things) My mercy can extend to *them.*

My child, you know that the only condition for My overflowing love and mercy is your *heartfelt sorrow* . . . and *always* sorrow that the wrong act should have hurt Myself. My forgiveness is instantaneous; you are made clean in My sight, worthy of My most tender care. Attendant evil influences are swept away. My child, that same love will now help you to forgive, from your heart, all who have hurt you. This is My law, and must be obeyed. Release them into My love.

To convey the peace of forgiveness concerning *any* sin is why I gave Myself . . . I wish My children to be drawn back to Me with the *pain* of guilt removed . . . even if memory cannot be erased completely.

I am the Lord your God . . . merciful, gracious, and infinitely patient.

(Exodus 34.6)

6

It would be wrong to pretend that maintaining faith in Me will always be easy.

There is the greatest temptation to see earth's calamities and misfortunes as pointing to a universe without soul.

Whenever you are forced to conclude, even momentarily, that you are alone in a materialistic creation, then evil has secured what is always its greatest ambition.

The one *crucial* division in this world is not between fortune and misfortune, but between life based on Me and shared with Me – and life divorced from Me, leading to oblivion.

When events seem to point away from Me and lead you into doubt, that is the *very moment* to summon all your strength and to tell Me that, in spite of all, I am with you and can never fail you.

You cannot know the *power* of such a trusting word – spoken to Me in circumstances which cause you to doubt!

Whoever believes in Me will live!

(John 11.25)

My child, because I in-dwell you by My Spirit, I experience in the closest possible way, your conflicts, your longings, all which can cause you distress. Because I have travelled your road, there is, within the Godhead, infinite, tender appreciation of what you endure upon earth.

Because you have responded to My call, however imperfectly, I have made you *My* concern . . . When I see you in great need, My love and compassion are made most real to you. Each heartache, each struggle can be made to awaken the sense of need of Me, to deepen trust, to teach new truths.

It is only because I can see the ultimate blessing to you of pain shared with Me, that I can accept (though *never* unmoved by them) your earthly struggles.

Recognise love's transforming work in earth's darkness . . . See experiences of darkness melt, under My hand, into experiences (within My love) of security and of hope.

I am making everything new.

(Revelation 21.5)

My child, your time spent in My company impresses upon you, deeper than mere intellectual assent, that you owe everything to Me.

Yes, I brought you into being . . . foreseeing that event. My hand was upon your life long before your thoughts turned to Myself. You owe to Me your very existence *now*, in a world which, without My victory, would have been lost. Recognise in your care in the hands of loved ones and the kindness of friends, My prompting and My provision. See Me as the *origin* of everything with which your life has been blessed.

The sense of gratitude to Me is missing from the lives of so many. You have the tremendous privilege of being among those who can make glad My heart by your recognition of your debt to Me.

You could never, of course, repay that debt. All I ask is your thankful heart towards your Saviour, and your Protector.

I have called you by name; you are Mine.

(Isaiah 43.1)

9

$\mathcal{T}$rue knowledge of Me comes when I am *valued* . . . To place Me above everything else in your life is indispensable to your growth . . . causing you to *thrill* at the thought of Me, and to desire closer and closer communion with Me.

When you arrive at the blessed state of My being all in all to you, you also realise that this has not made any *less* precious those whom you love on earth . . . On the contrary, My place of supremacy in your life encircles those other ties, and means that the influence of heaven is in your relationships – making them pleasing to Me.

Even at times of disappointment, let there be that steady *resolve* that I should maintain first place; this will draw everything into a beautiful harmony, as life loses its conflicts and its vain striving. My child, enthrone Me in that highest place now, and rely on Me to ensure that everything flowing from this is unerringly right.

I came so that you may have life . . . **abundantly!**

(John 10.10)

*T*rust is so often formed by difficulties and setbacks; a trust which remains, even when My way does not bring the 'results' which have been sought, when that way is hard to understand.

Blind trusting, when no obvious advantage is gained, is the *real* trust which I require, and which I always honour.

Follow the way of trust in every area, every conceivable situation upon earth – each relationship, each encounter, each problem. Yes, complete confidence in Me – expressed in joy, thankfulness, and in recognition of My touch in seeming coincidences and unplanned encounters . . .

My plans for you are unerring and will triumph, as you trust the voice within which assures you (in spite of observed circumstances) that I *cannot* fail a trusting child! Give Me, often, the glance of utter trusting love.

**In quietness and in confidence
will be your strength.**

(Isaiah 30.15)

My child, let My peace *enfold you* . . . not looking at yourself but at Me! Consciously and frequently rest your spirit in that peace; it brings true healing, and is all that you need.

Eagerly desire My peace for its *uniqueness;* know that it neutralises long-standing hurts. Unless My peace works upon deep wounds, you are at the mercy of so much from the past – its pain revived.

Firmly refuse unloving ways, wrong ways, which would temporarily destroy My peace in you; refuse them in My strength. Do not 'analyse' whether you have My peace; just *know* that it is there, as you are careful to tread My way . . . and it will pass from you to My other children.

My Name – the Name of JESUS – brings peace; Say it to Me – in love; say it to yourself – to comfort your heart, unfailingly.

Do not let your heart be troubled, or afraid.

(John 14.27)

The true goal of your companionship with Me is finding the reality of the things of the Spirit. Sadly, many still see worldly things as having more substance than their spiritual origins.

In taking Me into your life, you are acknowledging that the unseen is of supreme importance. No human encounter or experience must ever be divorced from the abiding reality against which it is set. The sharpness of this world's disappointments is removed (even though one's heart may be breaking), when their impermanence is compared with the fact of Myself.

Realising the unseen gives a sense of proportion to the experiences which temporarily elate or crush the human soul. To see My kingdom as the *reality* of this existence, and every other manifestation as transient, wonderfully gives courage and steadiness in the dark places. Life's passing phenomena are *transformed* by the reality lying behind them. Find in the world's experiences a *spiritual* gain . . . kept secure for you in the realm of My love.

My Kingdom is not of this world.

(John 18.36)

My child, the sense of isolation experienced in trying to tread My way is a stage which I see as necessary for you. There is the temptation to feel that too much is being given up . . . to feel, even, that you have been mistaken about the rewards of the spiritual life.

You have My promise that the stage of feeling isolated, perhaps discouraged, is a very positive one in your growth. You will find that nothing (harmless in itself), which seemed to be coming between us, and which you have surrendered, will ever be the subject of regret. What I give to you is of infinitely more worth than earth's riches.

In what the world may see as isolation, you find companionship at the deepest level, a sense of being lifted through uncharted areas of difficulty. Affirm very strongly when tempted to feel discouraged, that I belong to you! . . . aware of being provided for in the fullest possible sense.

**I will go with you
and prosper all that you do.**

(Exodus 33.14)

Call upon Me when any hurtful or overwhelming situation arises – *firstly* so that you may learn the lesson I have for you in it; *secondly* so that I may break the pattern of events before it becomes too burdensome for you.

You know that I am more than equal to the things which may threaten you or make you anxious; they remain – by My permission – for as long as they can further My plans for you – and for others. For My loved ones I make every trial fit into My pattern, and to serve a good purpose; you know that they are not really trials if I *share* them and then *conquer* them with you. I have *used* life's experiences to teach you, to sanctify you, to give you victories.

None are more aware of life's pain than those who seek My way; yet My peace and joy are found upon that way . . . and My presence, the priceless gift which is to be sought above all else. As you pray about everything, you will increasingly be able simply to *watch* the answers to those prayers come!

In the world you will have trouble and sorrow ... but rejoice ... I have conquered the world.

(John 16.33)

*T*hose who have not experienced what I can be to them, can subtly take away My *supremacy;* these include some who claim to carry My name in this world.

My child, your confidence in Me will be undermined when I am, to you, anything *less* than . . .
>the source of all love . . .
>the source of all made things . . .
>the source of all power – interpreted
>for this world's needs.

To place your life into My hands is to receive all the resources of the Godhead; resources *focused* in Myself upon earth . . . so that My children would be drawn to Me as the fullest expression of the Father's love.

Let your spirit be gloriously uplifted many times each day by realising My almighty and never-ending *responsibility* for you.

I and the Father are One.

(John 10.30)

The almost instinctive speaking of My Name when life is dark and uncertain …
> the cry of a child for the One who can draw close;
> the cry of a child when reasoning ceases to function, when all is threatening, when human help is absent, when confidence is lost.

The speaking of My Name brings into the foreground of your situation the one vital factor. My Name can be said in helplessness… but said in joy and thankfulness only seconds later! Thankfulness at being brought through that state of helplessness.

The speaking of My Name ensures, immediately, the retreat of evil forces . . . acknowledging that they are defeated in their aim for your life.

My child, the whispering of My Name …On waking … On surrendering to sleep … And very frequently during each day!

**I will be with you
when you go through deep waters.**

(Isaiah 43.2)

There will be times when you will not see the immediate way ahead. You may be filled with panic, wanting to avoid what could be a disastrous step. Remember that you do not always need to see the road ahead. It is sufficient, for the moment, to see *Me!*

When the time is right for a choice to be made you will know and I will assist you through it. Until that time be sure that merely keeping close to Me guarantees your moving in the right direction, despite questions and doubts raging in your mind.

When you cannot see clearly the next step, there is a good reason for My withholding that awareness. It becomes a time of trust . . . trust, very often, that I will simply *cause* My wish for you to happen! Do not feel the awful responsibility of choosing your path when that is not necessary for the moment. Just hide in Myself and know that you will soon see clearly… Until then, you are *precisely* where I want you to be.

Your Father knows what you need.

(Matthew 6.8)

My child, a radical change is made in your life when you focus, clearly, upon one principal aim . . . to run through all your personal ambitions, all your relationships. The aim which will integrate your personality is a simple one: that in some way you will extend My Kingdom of love, even in situations which seem to contain formidable barriers against this happening.

Begin by deliberately bringing this aim to Me, for My blessing – even if you have made promises of this kind previously. I will have your aim before Me! I will honour that aim – not only on occasions when you yourself remember it, but when you are temporarily distracted from remembering it.

Each encounter with another person is under the influence of My Kingdom – to push back, a little further, those forces which darken this world. Thank Me each day that you are used to establish My rule of love.

Fix your mind on God's Kingdom and His justice above all else.

(Matthew 6.33)

$\mathcal{N}$ever admit that a particular area of your life is a 'defeated' one.

Because you failed, perhaps many times, in a certain situation, this does not mean that you must be resigned to defeat. It does not mean that victory was not very close.

My child, you will experience the joy of resolutely uniting yourself with Me, and meeting difficult places victoriously. No environment, no set of circumstances, need prove impossible for you, if you believe that My victory with you extends to *every* area. I look for that readiness (completely trusting Me), to enter, once more, those scenes of crushing defeat, and *this* time to prove that on all previous occasions you could have been a victorious person!

Any area of compromise, or of resignation to defeat, weakens the whole. See how many areas of your life have become, already, the scene of new reactions, new gains . . . Let this encourage you about the victory which can be yours in each remaining problem area.

With God, all things are possible.

(Mark 10.27)

See communion with Myself as your *highest activity;* . . . there are no places on earth where this activity is impossible.

It is no mere escapism, no flight from reality, to give time to the interaction of our spirits; it gives My heart the joy which compensates for a world following so many illusions. Your time with Me is one of trust . . . trust in My answering of your prayers; of giving Me room in which to work; of letting Me help you to profit from the lessons of current circumstances.

Temptations to restrict the activity of communion with Me are often disguised as 'pressing duty', and often involve misuse of time which will contribute nothing to your progress.

My child, *treasure* time spent, consciously, with Me, as I supply need for the hours ahead. Such communion, far from mere escaping, is *dynamic* in its essence . . . and is indispensable for you. You were not meant to live without My resources!

Only one thing is vital . . .

(Luke 10.42)

As a very necessary discipline, give to Me every set of circumstances with which you feel unable to deal. The pressure upon you to 'respond' to those circumstances may be great, but you must make time (even if only moments), in which to give the situation, with its uncertainty, its complexity or its fear-capacity to Myself.

The simple, almost mechanical, giving to Me ensures the Divine activity; the most fleeting moment spent giving a situation into My hands is repaid many times over by the moulding of events under My power and wisdom.

Always react, *firstly,* by giving difficult or distressing circumstances to Me; then patiently watch My oversight, and My intervention, in their development. What is urgent and necessary, involving your action, I will always show you. But your walk with Me must always be one of calm and patience, based on My *sufficiency.*

I am with you to save you.

(Jeremiah 1.19)

My child, let Me cut those cords binding you to earthly things which do not serve My purposes for you, enabling you to be 'lost', in the light of My presence; enabling Me to become everything to you.

You can live in heaven with Me *now*, enjoying its resources with which to transcend earth's limitations, and evil's strategy. Remain in that heavenly sphere in the midst of life's details.

Let your life be one in which you are conscious only of love and trust towards me. Let there be a continuity of praise and worship (in which I am always receiving from you, and you from Me), until the day when I bring you into fullness of joy in My presence. Look away from all temporary conflicts, and feel the peace which the day of your eventual fulfilment gives to you *now*.

Let your satisfaction be in knowing Me.
(Jeremiah 9.24)

You wonder why, after intense effort, there is not that assured and relaxing sense of My presence . . . Sadly, in many of those who follow Me, ways hurtful to Me have become habitual… their continuance seeming almost to be a *right*.

Every dark thought, every unloving word or action must *immediately* cause you to grieve over it. All that comes between us is best shown up against the background of My love. If My love fills your thinking, the ugliness of what can, from time to time, be in you is clearly seen.

If you fail to come to grips with ways of darkness and seek pardon and cleansing immediately, there are two results: firstly, a destructive and festering uneasiness deep within, which no 'justifications' can remove; secondly, the clouding of My presence, making the walk with Me, which you so desired, have no real substance. Do not permit, knowingly, anything which can hold up My purposes for you.

**Happy are those with pure hearts;
they shall see God.**

(Matthew 5.8)

𝔄lthough the way is narrow, it embraces many avenues of freedom. Once My will is assented to and set before you as life's goal, you find that My way is *not* one of restriction.

As your choices harmonise with My wishes for you, you experience a real freedom. So *much* is yours! Once wrong ways are excluded, and the narrow way is walked in My light, you discover undreamt-of by-ways. Along these by-ways there is heightened experience of what, without Me, is tarnished or productive of conflict.

Many fail to see that the narrow road to My kingdom is a liberating road . . . on which you enjoy a wide spectrum of blessings, which you can go forward and take.

My child, you may feel that you are not carrying all before you! In the worldly sense this may be true, but, having sought Me, you can be sure that My Spirit is taking you forward – and it is always the *best* way forward.

If the Son sets you free, you really are free!

(John 8.36)

My child, try to see, in the midst of life's trials, not merely the calmer waters which you feel must be beyond them . . . try also to see those trials as *actually serving* to throw into sharper relief the period of sunshine, and gratitude to Me, which must follow.

The agonising periods of existence, which would almost make you lose your hold on Me, can serve a very relevant purpose for you . . . otherwise I would not permit them. Pain is the raw material from which can be made a soul increasingly sensitive to My love's existence.

Life's pain and sorrows, allowed within My purposes of love, are constantly used to create what is ultimately noble and strong and of the heavenly sphere; they thus give deeper meaning to the great miracle of existence itself . . . the miracle that *I am*, and that this is a universe in which My love will triumph.

Your sadness will be turned into joy.

(John 16.20)

My child, each night deliberately hand over *everything* to My control. Let Me guard those deep places in you; permit My good influence to work.

I shield your inmost being. Rest, as a child, in My love and My greatness. Thank Me that, as you rest in Me, I will deal with all that would spoil your peace . . . harmful memories, disturbed feelings.

Do not strive. Do not watch yourself anxiously... just keep your attention upon your Friend! Be concerned about others' needs and trust Me, naturally, concerning yours.

Secure in My love, this and every night, let your thoughts centre, always, on My almighty power. You realise how precious is your assurance of My love for you . . . rest in that assurance.

I will give you rest for your soul.
(Matthew 11.28)

My child, promise Me that you will never abandon Me as your one supreme hope. Remember that promise, often, as a fixed point in your life. I will be very aware of your promise, as I reveal to you what life can mean in My care. I will be conscious of your promise even at your times of failing Me.

In failure, remember that in *My* heart there is a continuing trust in you to move on towards My blessings. Yes, I am able to see in *you* a reflection of My own faithfulness – even at your times of failing Me! You will always be conscious of broken promises. Although hurt by these things, I have made provision for your being uplifted and renewed at times of failure.

Be sure that everything you do takes for granted *My* simultaneous work on your behalf. Because I am there loving you and using you, let peace and hope *always* triumph over that needless anxiety or alarm. After failure, rise to new and exciting horizons, and enjoy the blessed sense of My *companionship* on your walk.

I am the Lord your God . . . your Saviour.

(Isaiah 43.3)

My love cannot be experienced, deeply, unless I have *shared* with you the sense of failure, the realisation of the world's emptiness and its deceptions.

My child, as we meet, together, the darkness which comes over a human soul so frequently, My response to the sharing-opportunity which you gave to Me is that of overwhelming you with a sense of My love; earthly things (previously so 'certain', so indelible) fade by comparison.

Excluding Me from any circumstances – either because of self-will, or momentary doubt of My *relevance* to those circumstances – deprives you of My love's uplifting power. The lasting certainty of My love will not have been learned in life's phenomena, but in places where, at first, My love seemed to have no meaning. Sharing deepens *conviction* . . . about the love always met in Myself.

The Sun of Righteousness will rise upon you with healing in His wings!

(Malachi 4.2)

29

Life will hold so many disappointments for you.

Your first thought, following a disappointment, must be that I have allowed it. Then, you must realise that I allowed it, *knowing what the future holds for you.* Give to Me all the hurt, the sense of being at the mercy of fate. Surrender, too, fear about how you are going to live with the disappointment. I will heal this for you. See life's reverses as obstacles put in your path by evil, to divert you from My way. React by showing your trust in My victory, by remaining calm and hopeful in My love.

Instead of being shattered by disappointments, remember what I frequently save you *from.* This is no mere false consolation, but My permitting only what I see is best for you. Therefore, accept present circumstances as the answer to your prayers of surrender to My will, and thank Me for them. Refuse *all* disturbed feelings when disappointments come and ambitions fail. Instead, *use* them to win, with Me, a wonderful victory.

Your heart will be where your treasure is!

(Matthew 6.21)

You cannot know why you were chosen, why you were drawn to seek my acquaintance... you realise that your being chosen was not for any merit . . . as all My servants have realised! Just *accept* My choosing of you, and feel very humble that I saw, in you, one whom I could lead to eternal life.

When the clouds of life threaten, as they must, often, for My chosen, see them as *part of* that drawing to Myself which you have now accepted as your destiny.

My child, thank Me every day for choosing you. See what that has meant, so far, in deepening faith, in knowledge of My ways, and in a sense of purpose. Understand that the process of being drawn to Me *must* continue . . . because it was a process which was established by My choice, long before you realised that choice! My promises are for you; claim them.

Because I chose you, I will wear you as one would a signet ring.

(Haggai 2.23)

In so many ways I have revealed Myself.

For this world's need, a *unique* glimpse of its Maker had to be given... a revelation limited in time, but unlimited in its effect and in its drawing-power.

You cannot know the nature of My revelation *beyond* your sphere . . . in My creation as a whole. Just be sure that, in your world, *truth* was disclosed . . . both about the power and about the love residing in Me . . . that disclosure transcends all man-made searchings after truth, and all supposed 'insight'.

Never accept that My revealing of the Godhead was partial, conditioned by human limitations in receiving. What was seen in Me was the true nature of the moving force in creation – with the all-important truth that everything is *love-inspired.* My child, do not look outside My revelation to your world . . . it is all that you need to know for this present life; no conjecture, no reflection, can add to it.

All things are given into My hand by the Father.

(Matthew 11.27)

It is not mere chance that the sense of My love seems to be accentuated when a child of Mine turns to Me from a loveless environment... I seize that opportunity to bestow the gift beyond price ... a love-sense which is peace-giving, life-giving.

There is a temptation, even among those who follow Me, to feel that a sense of My love and companionship is to be an 'addition' to earthly love and security. There is doubt whether experiencing My love is enough, in itself, when other loves are missing!

Through the ages, the ache for love in so many hearts has been more than filled by Myself. If life leaves you with no human love or understanding, rejoice in the completely *sufficient* awareness of My love ... meeting every *real* need. My child, I want you to be truly happy in My love, and I want many to find that love through you ... I know that, in this, *you* will not fail *Me!*

I, Myself, am the wealth which you need!

(Numbers 18.20)

Hope placed elsewhere than in Me – and there are many false beckonings upon earth – will always prove futile.

You may experience, at times, conflict which is unbearable. The world will be seen as an alien place . . . even, at times, bringing the desire to pass from that world. In those dark periods, let the hope which lies over your future *project itself* into your present. Discipline yourself to see life against the background of My eternity, enabling you to endure (joyfully) the inevitable intrusions of darkness.

My child, life can be progressively more difficult, especially for those who do not know Me. *Your* privilege is knowing that, with Me, that pattern is reversed. I save the good wine until later!

With Me – and *only* with Me – the best is yet to be.

Whoever has the Son has life.

(John 5.21)

Being united with Me involves a sharing, to some extent, of My suffering . . . the loneliness, the pain, the hostility and coldness of others, but also means being *completely victorious* over all that is of evil.

> it means reflecting Me . . .
> it means that I touch those with whom
> you are in contact . . .
> it means true serenity . . .
> it means a joyful hope.

Our closeness means that it is to Me that people in need come; it is against Me that evil tries in vain. You can now display a strength never previously shown, as you *see* us as united, as you let My love give you a victorious existence.

Dwell, often, upon your being united – permanently – with Him who created you! Let this unity make all the difference to your life.

Without Me, you can do nothing.
(John 15.5)

My child, each day try to recapture the *wonder* of my love for you . . . a love which could not be stronger. Merely acknowledging My love, with your life not *stirred* by it, is a parody of what a child of Mine should be.

To dwell upon My love is no idle self-indulgence, no self-comforting; it is at the very centre of your new life with Me . . . everything radiating outwards from it.

The wonder of My love for you – just as you are – and your consciousness of how much I have had to forgive . . . This is the driving force behind your spiritual advancement, and your reaching-out to others.

You have found that there is no love to compare with Mine . . . a love which can, at times, be felt *even more strongly* when you know that love has been hurt. Let My love never cease to amaze you . . . and make you ready to meet anything which this life can produce.

Even the hairs of your head are all counted.

(Luke 12.7)

To walk in My ways, you must start from the fervent *desire* to please Me; kindle that desire, see how vital it is, and mobilise your forces around ensuring that My will is done in your life.

You know that the actual yielding to My will, the conscious assent to it in any situation, *automatically* releases the power needed to carry it out. Ways existing throughout your life I am able to change for you!

Each day gently tell Me "Your will be done, Lord." Growing in this attitude of happy submission, you will find yourself, quite naturally, refusing everything contrary to My purposes for you. *Applying* My word will always hasten the perfecting of My plans for you.

That desire to please Me, combined with trust, will mean a new and victorious walk. My commands are no impossible ideal but that which we can accomplish together. Trust My word of love!

Take My yoke upon you.

(Matthew 11.29)

As you wait upon Me, picture My *reaching out* to you; this is the true way to see our relationship.

Reaching out to bring you, increasingly, into Myself, to be more firmly established within My love.
Reaching out to lift you from danger; reaching out to welcome you back after failing Me.
Reaching out to encourage you to leave the past (even the immediate past) behind; reaching out to encourage you to feed upon the thought of Me; reaching out to supply you... knowing that nothing which is for your ultimate good is withheld from you.
Reaching out to share the attributes which are My own . . . lending you a vision of the truth which is Mine, giving you courage, peace, and a heart which truly can love.

The reaching out is one of support *now*, that you may live in a completely new way, and leave behind, permanently, whatever has obscured your vision of Me.

The water I give you is a well, springing up into eternal life.

(John 4.13)

My child, learn *acceptance*.

So often you will be disappointed when the seemingly wrong person meets with you, rather than the one you had hoped for. You must see that the person you met was the right person *for that moment*. When things planned seem unduly delayed, or fall into place in what seems to be the wrong order, see, again, My over-ruling.

Completely trusting Me, you can expect a perfect attention to detail concerning places and times. Delay and uncertainty are of *My* ordaining . . . to develop trust, and reliance upon My wisdom. Thank Me for those 'inconvenient' or seemingly unproductive meetings; thank Me for the delays, after surrendering to Me. See how the things which you and I desire, occur at the most appropriate stages of your existence.

Acceptance, and gratitude, will make My activity very clear to you. Whatever comes to you as you live quietly and obediently is right, and is blessed by Me!

I will not fail you.

(Joshua 1.5)

There are many, many joys in My hand, transcending earth's joys by an infinite amount... joys experienced through the medium of this world, but originating in Myself.

Willingness to tread My way means that joy is there for the taking . . . bound up with the peace which comes to the obedient heart. My child, I command you to be full of joy! Rise above earthly things and know the gladness of being hidden in Me, immune from surrounding hurt.

Do not grasp at the world's pleasures in order to fulfil the natural human desire for happiness . . . your basic joy is in My companionship, My faithfulness. Let joy *break forth* in you – away with guilt and fear! Deep in your heart you *know* that all is well – let *every* part of your life now express this.

**No-one will be able to take
your joy from you.**

(John 16.22)

$\mathcal{A}$lways remember the element of *victory* running through My plan for mankind . . .

My power was first seen in subduing chaos, and then in bringing man to the place where he could see and know the divine. My very appearance upon earth was a victory – a victory of love – love desiring the emptying of self, in order to draw alongside My children. Forces of darkness were confronted by that victory during My earthly life and were scattered; they staked everything upon the climax of the Cross and were, again, defeated.

And now, My child, in your own life, My victory is perpetuated. Even the smallest gain is an extension of My victory – which is always there to be used. In My Kingdom of light lies truth, peace, affection, generosity, wisdom; in the opposing realm lie fear, error, impulses of aggression, all the seeds of human unhappiness.

In spiritual warfare you are privileged to be My servant, equipped with My weapons!

. . . given power from heaven . . .

(Luke 24.49)

The victory which I won for you provides that which the human race does not naturally have . . . the *power to choose*. This freedom used, always means victory. *You* complete My victory in the world.

If you earnestly wish to leave old ways behind I lift you above them! You can take My hand and step out into the realm of freedom . . . where I am fully in control, and in which there is great blessing for you.

Your very look to Me establishes that freedom, which is best exercised within the framework of single-minded obedience to My wishes . . . not partial obedience. Let there be an adventurous, utterly-trusting walk in the freedom I give . . . a walk in step with Me. Let My name be glorified by what you are seen to be. My child, allow Me to lift you, *now*, into that realm of freedom.

I am the way.

(John 14.6)

My child, you could not calculate the influence emanating from just one soul which is closely linked with Myself! From such a relationship there flows so much. My spirit works in each contact – and is then at work through a wider and wider field beyond.

The Spirit is contagious; it cannot help but leap out into someone's heart from a committed child of Mine. Love breaks down every barrier, and because the Spirit is simply love in action, a positive influence goes out from one who trusts Me.

When thanking Me for a valued meeting, however brief, thank Me, also, for the *continuing work* of My spirit, through and beyond that other person . . . an unbroken activity. My Spirit achieves what mere words could never achieve… proceeding from you to kindle in a despairing person, a new hope, a new resolve. However modest you may feel our relationship to be, My Spirit in you ensures that any hesitant, trusting relationship with Myself becomes wonderfully enhanced.

My Father is glorified by your bearing much fruit.

(John 15.8)

My child, you will have experienced that sense of joy and relief of reconciliation – perhaps on someone else's initiative, perhaps on your own . . . For a while you walked on air, because not only had the barrier at the human level been removed, but its removal lifted you into the realm of love, which I control.

When you experience the joy of reconciliation, when love and affection can flow again, you are very close to the mystery of My love, which is its essence. Hurt to Myself, or ethical failures, cannot affect the burning desire for an out-pouring and a receiving of that love.

True reconciliation is one of life's highest experiences . . . one in which you have come near to the heart of the love which many still fail to realise or to understand. Always seek to be reconciled; My prompting also means My strengthening!

Be at peace with one another.

(Mark 9.50)

There has to be a stage in your growth when you know that you have renounced the world, so that you can *love* the world! . . . It is only when all on the human level – however precious, however worthwhile – is seen as subordinate to Me, that you can embrace the world in all its aspects.

Self can intrude in whatever role you adopt in the world, unless I have infiltrated your affections and your judgement . . . you do not love others in a way which reflects the divine love until you have first 'distanced' the world, in order to embrace Me. If My love for you is always in the foreground then the world can be *received,* can be responded to. Remember that love is not just a comforting emotion, and that it can be costly. When you act lovingly, against 'inclination', you truly are carrying out My will.

I always use your closeness to Me . . . expanding My work in many different ways . . . Your closeness *is* service for Me, simply because My influence goes out from you!

I must be first in your affections.

(Exodus 20.3)

45

Never underestimate the *power* which is contained within My love's influence . . .

If you are directed towards My love, allowing yourself to receive, it is a change-bringing influence. When My love is sought, after failure, its influence can create peace and hope; it is victorious over opposing influences and sweeps away all fretfulness of spirit.

My child, see not only My loving 'attitude' towards you, but see My love's conquering *influence,* also directed towards you! Evil forces are dispersed, under *any* circumstances, by your openness to that influence. Carried in My love is healing of the spirit which no other agency can bring.

When circumstances threaten, allow the Divine love to exert its influence . . . preventing further harm. Remain in the light of that love, as harmful factors are systematically robbed of their power to affect this present stage of your life.

Simply go on living in My love.

(John 15.9)

There is always a crucial time in the building of a relationship with Myself. Forces opposed to Me will do their utmost to instil the suggestion that trust in Me is misplaced, and need not be pursued. Many have abandoned a life with Me at this point, or have wasted many subsequent years before I could woo them back to Myself.

Those early stages of trust in Me must be *built upon,* leading to My gift of the kind of trust which is unshakeable.

By what you are, and what you say concerning Me, help many to persevere in the one trust which proves to be life's answer.

Whoever maintains trust in Me has *life.* It is only when a sense of closeness is, for the moment, lost, that there is a realisation of how *unique* is that possession.

Will you also go away?

(John 6.67)

My child, I will never be swayed from My purposes by the fortunes of life. Life is transformed by fixing your sights upon Me, and by trusting My faithfulness.

The ground which you tread with Me is not always *easy* ground, but it is *safe* ground . . . it is the way forward, planned by Me, according to your individual needs. My intervention, My provision for you, are based on knowledge of your life's pattern which is Mine alone.

When discouraged, My children will always turn back to Me – showing their deep realisation that there is nowhere else to go but to Myself!

Your prayers – offered, so often, when feeling utterly defeated, but offered *trustingly* – are being wonderfully answered!

I will remember My promises.

(Genesis 9.16)

My child, as you gaze into My countenance, see the eternal question – "May I come in?"

There is, on My part, an unchanging desire to fill you, increasingly, with My presence. My longing to fill you did not cease when you first invited Me into your life. As you look to My love, you will always see a yearning for our *closer* identification.

The enhancing of My influence in your life – driving out ways of self – must always be your desire. The very look of surrender to Me, willing to submit to My love, is an opening of the door... leading to a human life which shines with the divine life.

Each day respond with an ever greater "yes" to the entrance of God into every aspect of your way of living.

If anyone opens the door, I will come in.

(Revelation 3.20)

There is great danger in thinking that you can admit or reject wrong things indefinitely – at will. Gradually your defences are weakened, as you tolerate what is wrong, feeling that it is only for that occasion . . . Eventually, states which are beyond help can be reached. Heed My solemn warning.

Progress is slowed immeasurably when you allow exceptions; precious gains achieved with Me are needlessly thrown away, your new status weakened, the way open to yet more lapses. See each exception as *hurting Me,* and let this help you to avoid them.

Do not let evil rob you, throwing you back into former ways . . . there is always a price to be paid for weakness when you could have been strong! If you wish to leave sinful ways *permanently* I would not in any way fail you. *Your* failure would be that of wavering in your trust.

**If you keep My commands,
you will live in My love.**

(John 15.10)

Carried in My love for you is a *wistfulness* about what you can give to Me . . . in a world largely forgetful of Me!

Never feel that you have little to give to Me. Every response gives Me great joy, great comfort . . . each response of gratitude, of childlike trust, of resolve to keep close to Me. These things may seem small enough to you, but they meet My *need* of your love-response.

Often your motivation will not consciously be that of giving to Me, but when our spirits are united on *any* matter, it is deeply and gratefully felt by your divine Friend.

Every God-ward turning, even with your own need uppermost, is a meeting of the Divine longing! . . . the beginning of your own needs being met, but also bringing to mankind's Saviour a very precious moment.

. . . do you love Me?

(John 21.17)

You do not merely 'look towards' the light of My presence. The light is more *immediate…* an encircling light, to be constantly visualised as the way in which you exist in Me.

Mine is the light which the powers of darkness know well, signifying to them that they cannot harm, or permanently impede, the course of My chosen one.

You have the privilege of refusing all that is of darkness. *Choose* the light instinctively; let it pierce the dark places in you; let it banish anxiety; let it help you to react rapidly against what should not live in that light.

I give you what you need to now live in a brightness which can be *constant,* helping you to regain peace, to avoid impossible and self-conscious striving. It is not merely a light of exclusion! My light produces an unburdened spirit… full of hope and ready to meet whatever comes.

Light has come into the world . . .

(John 3.19)

There are many things which you could desire for others, although your knowledge is imperfect about what is best for them, especially in the long-term.

That for which you can always ask, with absolute confidence, is *My* first desire also; that desire is for someone *to begin to experience My love.*

Whatever the need as you see it, ask, above all, for that dawning of My love in a person's heart. Sure that this is My will, have growing confidence in the effectiveness of your prayer. You need not look for results here, but be content to thank Me that I am at work.

My child, you do not need convincing that a knowledge of My unchanging love wonderfully meets the various human needs – indeed, able to prevent many of those needs from arising!

Always be deeply grateful that you are My partner in bringing in My kingdom of light. I am constantly working – in, through, and around you, so be quieted in spirit.

If you believe, anything is possible.

(Mark 9.23)

*T*here can be self-erected barriers against receiving all that I have to give.

There are the more obvious barriers: unforgiven sin, resentment, the pride which is content to allow relationships to be unhealed. Then, there are the more subtle barriers, especially that of *spiritual reserve* . . . not really *expecting* of Me, not fully acknowledging My intimate involvement, and My intervention.

Spiritual reserve is very vulnerable to the assaults of evil. There is the danger of the *wrong* sort of self-reliance, rather than that invitation of Myself into situations. The greater the reserve, the narrower is the opening for My influence. Such reserve is corrected by asking Me for the gift of *child-like* faith . . . one which looks to Me with awe, and with an expectation which is completely justified.

Expect only the *best* from Me . . . reaching heights which once seemed a mere dream!

Whoever does not receive the Kingdom of God as a little child will not enter.

(Mark 10.15)

Realise the value of rest – shared, consciously, with Me; realise the *completeness* of what you receive as you step aside from the world's demands and anxieties and surrender to My presence.

Come *often* for rest, however brief the time available; give your concerns into My love. Think of yourself as a child – a *forgiven* child, where there has been sorrow over hurt to Me.

No human agency can give the absolute shielding of the mind which is the product of My love and of My conquest of evil, as I deal with the causes of mental conflict. Physical rest alone can only partially restore, because much can still disturb. It is when you rest in *Me* that things are seen in their true proportion . . . glimpsing a way through current difficulties.

Here, you come back into step with My ordered purposes; you bring others' needs to Me; you begin to *enjoy Me!* Thanking Me that I am restoring you, *helps to actualise* that restoration.

Come . . . and rest for a while.

(Mark 6.31)

Remember that the unpromising temperament or the seemingly 'impossible' circumstances only serve to show how much I can achieve! Your possession of Myself is all-embracing and brings with it an influence to ensure the meeting of the deepest needs of the spirit, those which I see as important for you.

My assurance about My being faithful is more than just an encouragement; it is to bring closer your heart into utter dependence upon Myself.

To remind yourself of My faithfulness, reflect each day upon My care, the guidance through dark places; the dangers (fatal without My presence), through which I have safeguarded you.

Reflecting on these things, you will then need no argument to convince you of what I am able to bring about.

Is anything too hard for the Lord?

(Genesis 18.14)

Fear will so often retreat where there is thankfulness! A thankful heart not only brings joy to Myself, but enables you to find a satisfaction with your life which stops fear *at its source.*

It is the thankful and worshipping attitude towards Me which lifts you above the fear-inducing inroads made by evil. If evil's lies and distortions are accepted, fear can become all-pervading. The *thankful* heart is, in a very real sense, saying that love *reigns,* and that all must be well. Fear then finds it increasingly hard to gain a foothold.

Make many occasions for telling Me, warmly, believingly, that there is nothing to fear – as your life becomes one of childlike gratitude and natural praise.

The Lord your God is a faithful God!

(Deuteronomy 7.9)

Learn to recognise thoughts which could grow into emotions hard to control. Evil will introduce idle (seemingly innocuous) thoughts, which would lead you into critical or resentful attitudes, or to forming a wrong intention.

Cultivate the *alertness* which sees what are not the loving constructive impulses from Myself, an alertness increased by saturating yourself in My presence, My word, and in the enjoyment of life's finer gifts.

Recognising temptation for what it is cannot be learned except by those whose lives are centred upon Me; you will be *more* conscious of evil's activity as My follower!

As you find yourself starting to go down a wrong road – to agitation of spirit, to anxiety, to 'self' in any form, glance to Me and let *Me* assume control. The saying of "Only *You* Lord" (thus excluding all that is not of My influence), will help tremendously in restoring calm and optimism.

The devil . . . is a liar!

(John 8.44)

My coming into this world, to reveal the eternal God within the time-process, represented the way I *always* come to hearts who will receive Me. I came, wanting only to bring My children to their true place of security… within My Father's love.

> I came where knowledge and worldly status did not matter . . . as I still do.
> I came where there was consciousness of need . . . as I still do.
> I came where there was a readiness to blindly follow . . . as I still do.

Today there are many comings into lives upon this earth … quiet, and always rejoicing My heart. My child, never cease to thank Me that I have drawn you to Myself. My coming into any life is its great turning point . . . just as My coming at Bethlehem was the turning point of all history.

I stand at the door and knock.

(Revelation 3.20)

Try to regulate your life to My own working, as you can discern it ... In creation, as you know, that work is gradual – often imperceptible – but moving unerringly towards manifestations of beauty, and an orderliness upon which you can depend.

Much that would enrich life is lost through failure to seize My opportunities, failure to recognise where I am leading onwards . . . My children moving too far behind Me!

But there are equal dangers in manipulating life *ahead* of My pattern for you. No need of yours is forgotten and My often gradual work is very *deliberately so* . . . based on My omniscience.

My child, I will make you aware when you are striving ahead of Me . . . when there is that disastrous combination of self-will and impatience. You can then return to *My* pace once more, and regain quietness of spirit.

My sheep hear My Voice and they follow Me.
(John 10.27)

You see in the natural world how, where there is love, there is the continuing desire to save the objects of that love from their own folly and blindness. My child, realise the privilege of participating in My power to *over-rule*.

Exercising your freedom of choice, you so often go astray – especially when you have impatiently failed to *share* with Me. There are inevitable painful sequels to this wandering – which are there to teach you. In a way which far exceeds protective human love, I so often intervene . . . over-ruling that which would not assist along My path.

Yes, you can depend on My love, to over-rule for you, but do not *invite* heartbreak, or shattering reverses, by ignoring the Friend who anxiously waits for you to *refer everything* to Him. Living without reference to My presence means *danger*. Though still in My care, your progress, your peace are so easily lost.

God, in your midst, is mighty.

(Zephaniah 3.17)

My spirit in you will develop (if you will allow it), many gifts – gifts which I can use. My Presence will mean a *heightened* expression, in you, of those human qualities which point to My existence.

Your growing love, patience, courage, self-sacrifice, will be available for My *other* children. You may not recognise the development of those gifts, but others will; they will be filled with wonder at what My presence in a life – (working sometimes from virtually nothing) – can achieve.

Everything that is achieved through the gifts I develop in you will be known for its *lasting* quality.

> Hearts won for me.
> Hope restored in darkened lives.

These will be *real* achievements, when seen in the perspective of eternity . . . My child, I tenderly bless you now, making you strong to bless others.

You are the world's salt!

(Matthew 5.13)

In the times of crisis which I permit, proceed slowly, conscious of how much I feel for you.

In those crises, just speak the *truth* from your heart – as I give you the opportunity. Avoid needless talk, needless striving; let prayer surround each contact with others. Close to Me, I will show you very clearly by *events* that I am at work.

Avoid temporary 'solutions' which weaken your reliance upon Me. Reflect upon the way I have brought you through past crises; this deepens your trust in My *present* sufficiency, and that trust will melt into a joy which may have seemed impossible for you.

There, when present storms and crises have run their course, stands . . . Myself! See *beyond* the crisis, the place where I have gone before you… the place of *your* victory.

Peace, be still!

(Mark 4.39)

It is not mere imagery when I express the essential part of My nature as being that of the Good Shepherd.

Understand that where a child of Mine is lost, it is from no mere obligation that I seek to rescue. The pursuit of a lost child is because I am *incomplete* for just as long as that child is not safely back in My arms.

It is infinitely sad that a lifetime can be spent away from the place of security – consciously resting in My arms. Love will always pursue even the most wayward child, even the seemingly most hardened, longing for that true remorse, a sense of My tender mercy, a turning from wrong ways.

The divine love, in its uniqueness, will always seek restoration of a precious object of its creation – no matter how the world may see the uncompromising tenderness of such love.

Joyfully, he laid it on his shoulders.

(Luke 15.5)

My child, learn to see reflections of Me in the familiar. The Divine image, in which mankind was made, is often obscured, but has not been lost.

In every sacrificial act, in every patient bearing of pain, or of others' imperfections, see a partial reflection of My love; in every act of forgiveness, in every thrill of reconciliation (yes, accepting 'blame' in order to secure it), see My love reflected; in every befriending of a weaker child, in every unwearying support for that child, recognise My everlasting arms.

In all innocent and uncontrived happiness, see something of the Divine joy; in each turning from the plausible to better things, see a little of the Divine holiness; in each prayerful and patient taking of a human initiative recognise part of the eternal wisdom.

My image in man is *still* seen and expressed, showing you how inevitable is the eventual destruction of all which opposes Me.

I will make man in My own image.

(Genesis 1.26)

I would never ask of My children that which is beyond them. Remember this when striving to overcome obstacles and temptations for My sake.

It is, of course, vital to refuse temptation *at once*... refused by the glance to Me, the glance of faith . . . taking you above what would be wrong, as you see Me surrounding and upholding you.

All that lowers your spirits – doubt of Me, discouragement, anxiety – represents temptation, from which the sin affecting others can so easily occur. Guard against evil working through tiredness, or causing you to focus upon the imperfections, the 'unreasonableness' of others. See the hand of evil in any state of panic.

My child, crowd out evil by immersing yourself, as far as you can, in what is good, beautiful, joyful, and innocent. You are *already saved* from evil's power!

**My strength is made perfect
in your weakness.**

(2 Corinthians 12.9)

Understand that you can never make too many demands upon My patient love. Consider again My love upon the Cross.

I did not draw back from Calvary and I still wish to pour forth My love . . . *comforted* when that love meets the need of a child in failure, or distress of spirit . . . *comforted* because My love is being *fulfilled*.

Constantly see the *sacrificial* aspect of My love... waiting to respond when you feel that your demands upon My patience have become unreasonable!

My child, when conscious of failing Me, when full of remorse, look at My heart of compassion... Yes, your failures do cause Me hurt, but I am hurt *even more* when you fail to recognise, and feed upon, the *largeness* of My love.

There is no greater love than when a person lays down his life for his friends.

(John 15.13)

My child, consider the privilege of living in My secret place. The very human self shrinks from the assaults of evil and the world upon it, but in My secret place all that threatens you (seemingly from within you or around you), breaks down as you use the realm of My love as your fortress.

Here you find *real* security; here you can, at times of great difficulty, surrender to My enveloping love, and let everything else just slip away!

In My secret place, you absorb the strength needed to go on… you receive enlightenment – or the patience which you need until new light is given to you.

For you, I am Shield, Saviour, Lover, Renewer of your spirit.

. . . alone with your Father.

(Matthew 6.6)

At times of uncertainty, look to Me for that awareness of whether *your* immediate influence is to be upon events, or whether your part is to watch events unfold!

The presence of fear will so often guide you, and you must act contrary to the fear. Do not let worldly considerations affect your direction. When the way ahead is not clear I *will* be leading you if there is absolute abandonment.

Wait on Me about each specific choice. When I show you a clear path, and, around it, the unclouded sense of My love, you must be decisive. I will not permit consequences which I cannot use; do not listen to evil and fear the consequences of actions after waiting upon Me. Even the 'doubtful' consequences will hasten My plans for you. The results of seeking My will are always *good* results in the long term, even if immediate consequences make you doubt!

I will both guide and instruct you.

(Psalm 32.8)

You have seen how adversity can break down barriers, and make it possible for a loving relationship to be born. My child, it was always in My plan that the darker experiences would result in our coming closer.

Think much of My patience in awaiting your recognition of My watching over you. Think also of My joy when My love towards you began to be met by your own growing trust towards Me.

All in existence is designed *to bring us together*. That is why so much which puzzles mankind is permitted . . . where it can unite a human spirit with Mine. My love undertakes for you in all possible circumstances. See My hand in any complex situation given wholeheartedly to Me.

Not only can you feed upon My love, increasingly, but there is a drawing by *Me* upon your own growing love and sheer dependence upon Me... In My arms of love, go forward as a new person, with a song in your heart!

I have loved you with an everlasting love.

(Jeremiah 31.3)

There are two dangers for those on earth who contemplate the spiritual dimension.

The first danger is that of *separation* . . . regarding Me as wholly-other and virtually unknowable. I become the subject of endless search, which, by its nature, must be inconclusive. The second danger is that of *confusion*… making no distinction between that which I indwell and that which is alien to the world of the spirit.

My child, you realise that the first of these ways of thinking creates a self-imposed barrier to knowing Me as immediate, as identified with, and as friend. The second way of thinking can create an easy 'tolerance' in which the *defined* sense of My being is lost. A sense of moral obligation is weakened, and love and worship wrongly directed.

Yes, love Me where found in My creation and in My other children, but let My place in your thinking be *central,* and never vague or diffuse. Your trusting attitude has a definite effect upon the Divine working, creating the conditions for Me to act for you in the best possible way.

I am the Bread of Life.

(John 6.35)

A covering of love . . . My love gives meaning to possibilities, choices, temperament, circumstances. So many of mankind's ills stem from hurts unhealed by that love . . . hurts expressed in hatred, confusion and failure. My love's influence keeps out that which would spoil your inheritance as My chosen.

> My friendship involves a tender *shepherding;* an infinite patience; My desire to bring you through every difficult place.

Against the background of My love, fear melts away and you can meet every demand. Let love be your life's motivation . . . so that life is transformed, so that you are not only comforted, but aroused to attempt great things!

**As the Father has loved Me,
so have I loved you.**

(John 15.9)

In overcoming all that is of darkness, think not only of My victory, but of My love!

To bring together the Christ-within-you and Christ-around-you . . . you must see light . . . the light of My love surrounding you, the light *within* you of My power . . . a natural consequence of My indwelling spirit.

The awareness which *conquers,* is a dual awareness:

My encouraging and indulgent love.

My victory, with which you are united, automatically, having taken Me into your life.

Look often at My creation . . . its beauty and order. See evil as the *intruder,* to take away human happiness and to turn hearts away from Me. See the light of My surrounding love and the light of My power in you as *one whole* . . . a barrier against those intrusions. See the march of My creative and loving purposes, as quite unaffected by the evil activities which I permit – in order to increase your dependence on Me.

. . . that you may be children of light.

(John 12.36)

Remember that you must not return, in kind, the treatment which you receive from others. Others may treat you cruelly, take advantage of you, slander you, over-ride you; frequently, this will be *because* you follow Me. Sometimes your sense of injustice will be even greater, because the person who opposes you is another follower of Mine!

See the temptation to lose My precious peace; let *Me* deal with any outrage, any desire for verbal or other revenge. You cannot know the circumstances which led to your being hurt, or whether something in *you*, provoked that hurt. Lift up the heart of the person or persons to Me... and if the sense of injury burns deeply, pray even more resolutely. Let Me bring healing.

The instances in which prayer has prevailed – and a child of Mine has blessed that time when he or she did *not* retaliate, are *countless!*

If you forgive others, you will be forgiven.

(Matthew 6.14)

Try not to let a day pass without a new area conquered.

Look at ways which you need to change, enjoying the freedom granted to you. Be very specific in letting a particular area be under My influence to produce new reactions. Remember the obedience-obligations which must match the privileges which are yours, in Me.

My child, you will always be conscious of many things which spoil your relationship with Me, our friendship.

Instead of being overwhelmed by the sense of how many aspects need to be put right, I want you, systematically, to confront each area of weakness and to make each day into an *overcoming* day, keeping that steady gaze upon Me.

You will not need Me to remind you of the need, then, to hold on to the character-gain which has been made.

My grace is sufficient for you.

(2 Corinthians 12.9)

My child, every moment which you set aside for Me has more than the obvious benefits for you. Not only are you receiving healing of the spirit, and light for your way, but such occasions will affect the atmosphere of your busier moments, when, perhaps, you are unable to focus, fully, upon Me.

Your deliberate making of time for our spirits to be in communion helps to enlarge My activity in your life, so that you become increasingly aware of My presence – even when there is much to pre-occupy you; this awareness ensures the death of self.

It will be My Spirit in you which causes you to give that momentary glance in My direction when life is turbulent, and when you need, desperately, the steadiness which comes only from Me.

Feed your spirit, alone with Me, whenever you can, and let this communion with Me carry over into life's most demanding periods.

**Wait upon Me, listen to Me,
and your soul shall live.**

(Isaiah 55.3)

When there is much at stake, evil will go to endless lengths to divert you from My path. Look to Me to make you aware when decisions of importance are being made . . . decisions which are important from the *Divine* viewpoint; otherwise, those choices may have been underestimated in their significance.

Evil knows what can flow from these turning points in your life. In view of the potential danger, claim victory over opposing influences in any matter which I show you to be significant for your progress as My servant. I will hold evil in check; claiming victory will be a reminder of both the danger, and of the need to keep close to Me.

Facing new challenges, new opportunities, thank Me, constantly, that I am forbidding all that would confuse or hinder your true advancement.

**If you follow Me,
you will not walk in darkness.**

(John 8.12)

My child, is there anxiety?
Is there depression of spirit?
Is there a continuing sense of guilt, in
spite of My forgiveness?

The *only* remedy lies in Myself. Meet these assaults of evil in an entirely new way, allowing my victory to guard the deepest part of you against their continuance . . . sense, instead, the calm, the return of hope, and the belief in yourself, which My presence brings.

You know that My power is invincible . . . use every occasion to strengthen your defences. See negative things as *unable to intrude,* as peace once again fills your being . . . I guard you from their re-entry as you continue to look to Me. You can surprise yourself with new reactions, as you trust in what I am doing for you.

The Lord will save; He will rejoice over you!

(Zephaniah 3.17)

Fear is a stronghold of evil, to be pulled down if you are to be used effectively. Fear resisted means a better 'climate' for victory over sinful ways . . . evil can cause less havoc. In the same way, resisting sin provides a better 'climate' for conquering fear.

Fear may compel you to act in foolish haste; drive you into a wrong self-condemnation; lead you into overwork and stress by taunting you with neglect of 'duty'; discourage you from allowing those restful periods which restore the sense of My presence; lead you to neglecting important things, in favour of what is marginal.

Give Myself and others your love, and *only* be afraid of clear rebellion against My will. Complete victory over fear is possible in *this* life. My victory is yours to use . . . what is impossible with men I can accomplish for you!

Little flock, you must not be afraid.

(Luke 12.32)

Through history My children have rested upon My faithfulness, releasing their spirits from insecurity and forebodings. Such faithfulness cannot be equalled upon earth.

Being so far above earth's limitations, I can *ensure* that My concern for you is translated into very practical, unerring, intervention in circumstances over which you could have no possible control. My provision will not fail in any single day; wisdom, therefore, is to live only for the present. Trust opens the gate of My supply.

Yes, My child, I am watching your concerns during those times when you, yourself, may be careless about them. I am fitting into My plan those tangled aspects of life which you have given to Me; the *events* of your life are all working for you!

Before My children call, I will answer.

(Isaiah 65.24)

My child, the ideal preparation for answered prayer is ensuring that your *whole life* increasingly reflects your trust in My love – and My power over all creation.

Seeking the help or the healing of those known to you, do not look for instant or superficial results... know that your prayer releases My healing power, and loosens any hold of evil.

Thank Me that the person for whom you pray has been *drawn closer* to me, and is *receiving*. Thank Me that all your prayers – made with my love and power firmly in your mind – are greatly used. Peace and hope will come to many others through you, as your trust deepens.

What a privilege to know that you are linked with My loving, saving activity among My children!

**Whatever you ask in prayer,
believe that you have it, and it will be so.**

(Mark 11.24)

You have found that there is a great gulf between expressions of trust (and even those genuine *feelings* of trust) . . . and the launching-out in trust.

You know that I am invincible. Sometimes, when this is put to the test (occasions when evil challenges you), you show the incompleteness of that trust. It is a wonderful victory for you when, full of misgivings about being able to act in a new way on *this* occasion, you trust My *invincibility* . . . and do so!

Trust is at the centre of all spiritual progress and must cover not only My general ordering of your future, and your safety in Me, but those fierce everyday conflicts where, so often, there is compromise, rather than victory.

My child, as you *act* trustingly, all that opposes Me in your life will surrender to My presence.

**If you act on My words,
you are like the wise man who built on rock.**

(Matthew 7.24)

My love must be brought against every jarring circumstance, every uncertainty, to inject peace.

You have found that your peace must never depend upon variable fortunes; use of My love in giving entrance to peace must become perfect. Before the cutting edge of circumstances can colour your mood, let My love exert its neutralising activity; before someone's troublesome ways or seeming character faults simmer harmfully inside you, invite My love.

My love literally robs life's demands and trials of their power to upset your balance. Let those fret-bringing circumstances be swallowed up in the thought of My love . . . never waiting for circumstances to be changed, either spontaneously, or by your efforts. Hold to the thought of My love until you *know* that whatever may have troubled you now has given way to peace.

If only you had known
that upon which your peace depends.

(Luke 19.42)

If, in dark places, your dutiful expression of thanks to Me seems unreal, remember that *your* gratitude is not restricted to life experiences; your gratitude extends to mercies yet unrealised!

Nothing brings more joy to My heart than your fundamental trust in My activity, when you can see very little cause for thanksgiving. You are then sharing in My own *anticipation* of what is in store for you. When thanking Me that I cannot fail you, you have entered the dimension where plans are constantly made for your greatest good ... the dimension where present darkness is seen as scattered.

My child, a life of thanksgiving and worship in the midst of what, at times, is totally discouraging, is something to which you are called. Thanksgiving reveals a human heart which understands, deeply, the *faithfulness* of the divine love.

It is your faith which has saved you; go in peace.

(Mark 5.34)

Nothing can take you away from My road except your *invitation* to those distractions!

All the time I am neutralising things which would send you astray, but by your self-will, temporarily adopting the world's standards, you can wander from the security and the upwards nature of My road. Although you can never go out of My care, you have surrendered so much … ground which must be recovered, often by a long, painful process.

Do not feel complacency, therefore, about remaining in My care and that the road can be rejoined, easily. Because of My love, much is restored immediately, when there is sorrow over things discordant with My wishes. But true wisdom is to *avoid* the need for the recovery of lost ground. Refuse all temporary compromise; avoid too lightly entering areas of danger by your words and actions . . . You can then depend upon Me to keep from you all manner of dangerous influences.

**Think of what I have commanded you . . .
and obey.**

(Joshua 1.8)

My child, see the nature of what can obstruct your way. You are aware of the evil activity which creates obstacles for you . . . human opposition, confusion, less-than-perfect confidence in My power to conquer with you.

With any seeming obstacle you have a choice: of going around or through; the factor common to both, of course, is prayer. Remember that an obstacle (real or imagined) is so often simply *taken away* by your prayer of patience and trust... a removal which owes nothing to your own initiative. When an obstacle *remains,* needing to be grappled with (a principle defended or courage called for), prayer is again your resource.

Not one apparent barrier to your spiritual realisation is ever permitted to remain – unless, temporarily, for a good purpose. Stand firmly upon Me as obstacles disappear, or as you surmount them with a strength not your own.

The walls of the city will fall down for you!

(Joshua 6.5)

My child, there is much misunderstanding about what is hurtful to Me. The greatest offence to My love is when there is a determination to follow an impulse which you know in your heart is not of Me. Failure to make reference to Me, and to adjust conduct, runs contrary to My constant and rightly-directed influence upon your future.

Falls are inevitable in the weakness of your human condition and, often, it is as if there was a conspiracy to catch you unawares. Failures of this kind, occurring in the complex area of relationships, and conflicting goals, are (because of My mercy and patience), *less* damaging to your eventual realisation than is deliberate self-will.

When I am temporarily 'put aside', My love is not withdrawn, but an influence for good is lost, and you can be ensnared in an area which is futile or wasteful. However strong the pressure to do so, never exclude Me; cultivate a wise fear of the ultimate hurt to Me . . . self will!

It is a broad way which leads to destruction.

(Matthew 7.13)

You will often feel that you wish to give to Me in sheer, joyful realisation of My provision in your life.

What can you give to Me?

At the very start, you must always have stood at the Cross, pondering My saving act for you, and whispered "Lord, my heart is Yours". Long before your good works or victories over wrong ways are established, the gift of your heart is not only accepted but *remembered* by Me . . . a gift often before Me.

My child, the decisive difference in your life is knowing that you are not your own! Find deep satisfaction in the fact of your heart having been given to Me. Occasions of bringing joy and comfort to Me – (your kindness to others, your witness for Me) will all flow from the indispensable initial gift of your heart.

You must be born again!

(John 3.7)

Because My children have a very real free will, I have ordained that there must be a conscious *effort* in obedience . . . against contrary pressures and desires. This effort is *always* blessed by Me. Obedience does *not* mean a strained conflict; rather, it is a joyful and patient walk in My way.

My child, be *lost* in My love, so that I may bring about My plans for you quickly. Keep your promises to Me . . . without inward debate, or concern about whether you 'feel' certain.

There is so much to do in those whom I draw to Myself. The secret of walking in obedience is always a *response* . . . to My love! Where I see faithfulness (despite failures), I reward that faithfulness by taking My children on to higher ground, where increasingly, My purposes are fulfilled in them.

**Hearing the Word of God and keeping it,
means true happiness.**

(Luke 11.28)

My child, ask that you will be able to distinguish, over a widening area, between what is of Me, and that which is tainted by evil. Sensitivity and the avoidance of what is harmful comes from being in My company, and from your determination to follow me.

There are deceptions of evil in spheres where much is at stake . . . including institutions which bear My name. Wishing to know what is of Me, and not to go astray from Me, you will emerge from confusion. You will not need to seek My will anxiously, but find yourself, instinctively, knowing what is of light, and following it.

Let Me make you vividly aware of danger – either in the situation around you, or in your thought processes, which precede action. If you *really* wish My warning voice to be unmistakable in a confused world, it will be so.

Walk in the light while you have it.

(John 12.35)

You see in My self-emptying, culminating in the Cross, the sacrifice which *you* may often be called upon to make . . . laying aside knowledge and pride, and becoming as a child. In that humble state, prepared to be exploited, prepared to *lose*.

See, in My self-emptying, the tremendous lengths to which love will go on behalf of its children. This, too, is *your* pattern. When you are emptied of self . . . all that is world-acquired, you can, most effectively, reflect Me. My self-emptying made it possible for Me to be *approached* . . . for My children to *expect* understanding. I could only meet My children at the level of their need by letting go everything but love.

My child, for you this will be costly . . . but there is no other way.

I am humble and gentle in spirit.

(Matthew 11.29)

How do you see those around you?

It is good for you to ensure, frequently, that, indwelt by Me, you are looking at the world with My love's eye. You cannot fail to see prejudice, callousness, greed, deception, coldness, in so many. Your awareness of what originates in the power of darkness will have been enhanced by My presence with you.

Seeing existence with greater clarity, you must now let My love permeate your judgements! It must become instinctive to see the 'unreasonable' person as one needing My blessing, and for you to desire that blessing. Do not injure others, either directly, or by vindictive conversation about them.

Instead of mounting anger about the shortcomings of those around you, feel My presence softening your attitude towards them. Obey My injunction to bless a child whom you *now* see in his or her *need*.

**What reward can you expect
from merely loving those who love you?**

(Matthew 5.46)

When you are terribly disappointed with yourself, and know that you have hurt Me, just turn to Me and know that you are not cast away.

Know that I still need you.

Know that because of your trust in Me, we are companions in this dark world.

Yes, although your failures are many, you need not lose hope, because the task of renewing your life *has been given to Me!* Acquire the great skill of resisting evil as the *new person you* are in My sight. *Effortlessly* allow Me to guard you, to give you immunity from evil's fiercest pressures ... thanking Me as you do so!

Be very teachable . . . and *apply* your lessons. Launch out courageously, centred upon Me, and I will ensure that you do not falter in your walk.

A mother may forget her child, but I will not forget you.

(Isaiah 49.15)

The return to Me.

It is not only in self-willed action and in conversation that you can stray from Me. I want you to learn the return to Me in the realm of *thought* . . . be so aware of Me that there is an instinctive loss of peace when your thought-processes carry you into areas of danger.

In the realm of thought, the seeds are sown for that which can produce great good – or for that which may be disastrous. Refuse to stray, so that the Holy Spirit may go on sounding.

It is in the area where My Spirit dwells – prompting what is good – that evil can try to divert you. Be very alert to thoughts which conflict with love, with patience, or with trust in what I am doing. *Return*, with immediacy, to My indulgent and welcoming presence.

A good tree cannot produce bad fruit.

(Matthew 7.18)

It is not only by those who move confidently that the race is won . . . it is so often won by those who move deliberately, almost tremblingly!

Do not be over-anxious about your spiritual progress. An apparent standing still in the world's eyes often hides a true advance . . . Even if progress seems slow, thank Me for it . . . Never *remain* in disgust with yourself, for this implies that My work in you is not going forward.

If your desire is to be perfect, you shall have your desire – and the details of the journey will be woven into My plan for you.

Those claiming to trust My greatness can still put Me to the test in a tense or doubting manner instead of taking Me for granted. Leave with Me the constant preparation work, the shaping of your soul for eternal life.

**I pray for them . . .
that they may be made perfect.**
(John 17, 9 & 23)

$\mathcal{A}$ prayer made from a heart which is becoming closer to Me will be made with growing confidence . . .

about My joy in your asking;
about My bringing about what
is right for you.

You can experience the answering of your prayers, increasingly, as our wills become united. You will see clearly what can be yours, that for which you are right to ask . . . all within the framework of a submissive heart, free from worldly objectives and hatreds.

I will show you *what* to pray for and *who* to pray for; you will sense My delight in granting the highest which you could ask on behalf of yourself or another. Even if, by human standards, My fulfilment of your requests may seem to be slow, it is the certainty of what will be achieved which is the important thing. Trust Me and thank Me!

**Your heavenly Father
will give good things to those who ask Him.**

(Matthew 7.11)

Love at the heart of all things – even those which distress or which puzzle you in My creation… see all that is discordant against the background of My love.

Let there be a place in your heart where the sense of My love is untouched by the events of this earth. My love is life's great place of safety, coming between the trusting child and the power of darkness in all its manifestations.

You will be increasingly sensitive to wrong – both in all that surrounds you, and in yourself. You will feel deeply that wrong, where once you merely 'observed' it. Sensitivity to that which darkens life, carries with it, also, a deepening conviction about the love surrounding all that you experience.

My child, thank Me for everything which has contributed to the realisation of this love.

Happy are those who have not seen Me, but believe.

(John 20.29)

My child, the greater your realisation of My love, the greater is the degree of healing present. Whenever My love is sought, there begins a parallel process. There is healing (both internal, and in your contacts with the world).

The advance of My love in you heals any sense of insecurity, heals any sense that life is something alien, something to be feared . . . You realise that the deepest human love cannot achieve this. Only *My* love can penetrate barriers to the wounded places.

As wounds are healed, My love's influence affects every ambition, every relationship – whether close or casual. There is healing, because all that would create disharmony has to retreat in My presence. Therefore, visualise the *light* of healing within you.

You may not always be aware of the healing process, but can take it for granted that *all* contact with My love brings lasting healing.

I am the Lord who heals you.

(Exodus 15.26)

Sometimes, the circumstances of life and My word seem so hard to reconcile; My counsels seem to be only an ideal – shattered by the realities of living. And yet, when My word is acted upon (often in blind, clinging faith), it proves itself exactly what is needed; it is the word of truth – all else is 'appearance'.

In My Word is found all the qualities of My Godhead . . . you touch My love, My wisdom and My power. *My* word is transforming, hope-producing – going to the heart of every situation; it always validates itself.

As you receive My word you can survey calmly circumstances which may be producing agitation or despair. You can look up from the surrounding darkness and sense My concern, My control of events.

Cherish My word – rest in it, bathe in it: let it unfailingly uplift you, steady you, and bring you courage.

**Heaven and earth will disappear,
but My word will endure.**

(Matthew 24.35)

Do not feel that there is a sharp distinction between heaven and earth. Heaven is simply the realm where the presence surrounding you here is experienced more fully . . . The bliss of *realisation*.

In the heavenly places are those souls whose acquaintance with Me began on earth – as yours has. Heaven is the reward, not for earthly perfection, but for *persistence* along the road of the Spirit, despite enticements to stray from that road.

The peace which blunts the sharpness of earthly pain and conflict is the peace of heaven experienced *now*. When that peace is experienced, earth recedes, its temporary opposition is forgotten. If you have grown in the conviction of My love for you, let that burn as a steady light – affecting the remainder of your life here. That light will burn, I do assure you, until the day when My presence is beyond all arguments and embraces . . . *yourself*.

The Kingdom of God is within you.

(Luke 17.21)

My children, looking for strength, so often forget that the power lives within them, and needs to be *used*.

When looking to the future with its many demands, and its potential for fear and sorrow, remember that for those demanding places, the strength of your Lord *is already within you*. You need never feel at the mercy of events!

It will become perfectly natural for you to draw upon My *nearness . . . at once . . .* finding courage, finding a thread of hope in some shattering reverse, finding a peace which defies the circumstances of the moment. Think of the hurt to Me when My strength is not used; think of My joy as we conquer together.

My child, so often the instinctive using of My strength would have helped you in what resulted as failure. I have had to lead you through many failures, to realise just how much can be overcome by banking upon the power which is *part of you*.

I will hold you by your right hand.

(Isaiah 41.13)

M y child, come . . .

Come ... with that sense of helplessness or
insecurity ...
Come ... when things are overwhelming...
Come ... to find all your needs met ...
Come ... simply to let My love *feed* you ...

The look to My love! . . .

dispersing fear;
dispersing that needless sense of guilt;
dispersing all turbulence of the spirit;
dispersing loneliness;
dispersing dread of the future;
dispersing regret;
dispersing sorrow;
dispersing any sense of rejection;

Is it not a wonderful thought that I can fulfil any
need for you? Keeping the sense of My love is
the secret!

I am He who comforts you.

(Isaiah 51.12)

Each difficult choice carries a potential…
for your growth! In trying to follow My way,
something of the divine wisdom has developed
in you . . . True wisdom (as distinct from mere
'reasoning'), is never in conflict with My
commands.

As you earnestly seek My way, your own
judgement, and the way which I seem to be
indicating, begin to coincide. The coinciding is
the result of a blending of our spirits . . . seen on
occasions of temptation (when you *know* what
you must do), and at times of genuine
bewilderment. Let each choice be dominated by
the thought of My love.

Avoid all that is of self-will, or of fearful haste, or
of disregard for others' feelings. Avoid turning
away from Me and acting compulsively. Each
wise spirit-guided choice involves a very
significant victory which you may not always
recognise at the time, but which is building up a
relationship able to carry all before it!

. . . leading you into all truth.

(John 16.13)

The highest points reached in your soul's development may not be those which you, or possibly those around you, see as such.

The times of real progress are when the pattern of your life comes closest to the pattern of My working . . . when there is nothing discordant between them. When there is this harmony between your spirit and Mine – often in a worldly setting which is 'unpromising' – then anything is possible, both in you and through you.

Many are deceived about where happiness lies. True joy steals upon your soul, unselfconsciously, when there is this unity of purposes; when love, in its deepest and many-sided sense, is dominant. Even those who do not know Me, and yet love, experience this harmony, to some extent, because it is a law of My universe. For those who know and trust Me, however, it is a state greatly enhanced . . . giving a unique sense of purpose and tranquility.

Be holy . . . for I am holy.

(1 Peter 1.16)

See My love as the starting-place . . . Much that is hard to understand becomes clear, as you contemplate all phenomena as love-motivated. Even earth's tragic elements, as you have found, can find a necessary place in love's purposes.

If love is traced as the starting place, so much of what has been allowed in your life will begin to be accepted. See My own attributes as having their origin in universal love. See love as the fountain of My wisdom, of My patience, and of My power in creating, saving, healing

When life's misfortunes threaten your trust in Me, resolutely refuse the abandonment of that trust. Reminding yourself that My love has allowed the misfortune will reduce the duration of sadness or of regret; you will then see, so often, how love is planning in the midst of the misfortune, that for which you will soon express gratitude.

God loved the world so much.

(John 3.16)

Move through life upon the promise that every obstacle *is already conquered for you!*... a result of the Divine omnipotence. Trusting in this truth ensures, automatically, My victorious influence.

Never hurt Me by doubt, when victory for you in *any* matter is so close . . . doubt of all that is promised to you is evil's ambition for your life. At the heart of doubt of My promises is doubt of Me. Do not see inevitable obstacles as needing to be faced, unsure of the outcome . . . see them as already removed if you accept My power and My wisdom. Nothing can stand in your way, with your hand in Mine .

The knowledge that I am active in your cause must continue to give you patience. You must still allow Me the space in which to work! If you are keeping close to Me, no circumstances are adverse. Yes, you can *enjoy* uncertain situations because you are in My care.

I am with you, wherever you go.

(Joshua 1.9)

My ways are patient ways. They *must* be. So much has to be held together in My creation and fulfilled according to My wisdom. Let *your* life be a copy (within your limitations), of the Divine activity – in its *sureness*.

Evil would obscure from you the *real* state of things – My eternal perspective which, increasingly, can be yours. Limited vision could lead you into hasty action, anger, folly, and even self-destruction.

Many things are desirable, but not all have to be undertaken immediately. Only that which is blessed by Me is truly effective . . . those things in which *you* show patience prove worthwhile, because I complete them. Let *My* activity give you both restraint, and an eager looking-forward. 'Results' may not always be seen immediately!

Covet the *Divine* perspective . . . achieved by a life closely involved with My own.

**To bear fruit,
the branch must stay united with the vine.**

(John 15.4)

You realise how the pattern of your life can be completely changed by a single event, and yet the world, sensing this, still does not turn to Me as its stability. I stand willing, in My love, to minimise the inevitable and frequently heartbreaking changes which life brings.

A life divorced from Me has nothing, when its way is suddenly shattered by earth's events. And yet a life whose foundation is Myself still has *everything,* even when the loves of earth are taken, or its ambitions crumble.

It is against the background of that which is unchanging – Myself – that life, which is intrinsically one of change, must be built. To seek Me early, when the world is secure, is wisdom… and yet, that desperate *late* turning, when all seems lost, is always met by My love.

If life is difficult and uncertain it does not mean that you are no longer on My path; you remain on that path because of your *trust!* Rejoice that your life is involved, increasingly, with My existence.

I am . . . Life.

(John 14.2)

Even when sharing life with Me, there occur doubts – occasioned by the phenomena of My world and by the tremendous suffering, waste and futility with which creation is burdened.

Such doubts are intensified, almost unbearably, when darkness descends upon one's own life, or the life of someone dear; one may be completely unable to see beyond the darkness.

Remember that pain is never My will and that I am never remote from it. Pain and anger mean pain unrelieved and utterly wasteful; pain shared with Me means the entrance of light . . . a *changed* situation, even if it 'appears' merely to continue.

In bringing good out of chaos, I am *very much at work* in the world's drama of alternating light and darkness. I am using *precisely this* sort of world to bring about the spiritual gifts of compassion, patience, bravery and appreciation of Myself. The only qualities which will ultimately matter.

Whoever endures to the end will be saved.

(Matthew 24.13)

Sharing My life, you will see more deeply into the complexities of human behaviour. Earth's blindness results from the activity of evil. So often, men have acted upon a lie, when to turn to Me would have saved countless tragedies.

I have granted to you to look upon others with the love I have for them. Now, let Me also lend to you the eye of *truth* . . . Realising My presence will help you to see beyond the superficial . . . You will *understand* . . . You will be able to reject false attraction; you will see the *lostness* behind someone's anger with you.

My child, love to see My truth in life's phenomena and resist any pressure upon you to act, even momentarily, against the truth which you know. Be sensitive to any clash between My will for you and the signals which the world gives, as you expose yourself, inevitably, to it.

The truth will set you free!
(John 8.32)

My child, do learn tranquillity in adverse circumstances, without fretfulness to see those circumstances changed at times when they cannot be.

As soon as you realise that those circumstances are working to your advantage, there is the onset of peace. Only I can bring this about for you, and trust must be absolute, (transcending natural human reactions), that I *am* at work in any situation which I permit.

As you accept what cannot be changed, your courage is greatly developed, and your dependency upon Myself strengthened. You will learn to be completely independent of circumstances . . . their fluctuations leaving you untouched.

Keep constantly in mind that you have life's one gift beyond price . . . In My love, turn your back upon earth's fret-bringing events. Resist the continuous pressure by evil with strength which is also continuous!

. . . that in Me, you might have peace.

(John 16.33)

Everything can speak to you of My love, if only you will listen with the Spirit's ear.

My presence with you, My love for you, are the things in which you rest . . . they encircle your life. Think much of the *indivisibility* of the trusting child and its Maker. My gift to you is the sense of My nearness. This sense must touch every aspect of your life ... Always see, in Me, the One who has promised what no-one else could, able to convert those promises into a wonderful reality; they are not too good to be true! My promises are not lost by human failings, provided that, in sorrow over failure, My path is resolutely taken again, with a reaching-out to Me for renewal.

Tell Me at the start of each day of your intention to keep in the way which I have shown you. My way, applied to the *details* of that day, will then be increasingly clear to you. Make use of all that I have given you. Are you trusting My promises? It is that or nothing.

**I will never forget you – your image
is on the palms of My hands.**

(Isaiah 49.16)

In life's most frightening places you so often will find yourself sure of only one thing in the whole of existence – My love for you. But that will be enough! As a child, you rest in My love as the one thing which you can take for granted; yes, you can let Me *caress* you!

With the strength absorbed in dark places, you can anticipate many victories. Keep in the *brightness* of My love.

When you are conscious of evil's influence threatening to break you down, know that it cannot do so. Keeping hold of Me when things are dark, when tempted to doubt Me and to doubt My word, are your times of *genuine* trust. My promises *must* be realised; this is your stability in uncertainty.

Who but Myself could make something of the situations in which My children find themselves?

It is I; do not be afraid.

(Mark 6.50)

Bringing light into others' lives *must* be your aim . . . even when personally discouraged or weary! Let there be more *boldness* in what you attempt for Me . . . I will send opportunities, to be grasped in the spirit of adventure. Do not turn back from this call, whatever discouragement or hostility you meet. Be *available* for Me!

So many of My suffering or lost ones need you. As My chosen, My instrument, I strengthen you. What you cannot do without strain, I always undertake, completing your task.

I wish to do great work through you for My *unique* purposes. Make the conditions for My power to flow by an ordered and purposeful life.

Let Me give you a sense, deeper than human understanding, of people's needs. *Thank Me* that I have passed through you in some way . . . not always the way you could have anticipated!

There is a large harvest, but few to send.

(Matthew 9.37)

Your expression of hope in Me brings about two things: firstly, it helps you to acquire a sense of proportion about both the world's supports, and its demands; secondly, it sets free My love's provision, so that you can, uniquely, draw upon it.

Yes, you are tempted to fix your hope upon many other things – even after your decision to follow Me. You must resolutely picture the place of light – the sphere of My all-embracing love – as the focus of your hope in this life.

However precious and sustaining are this world's friendships, your *permanent* hope must be fixed in Me. However attractive are this world's rewards, they must never weaken such hope. Your daily walk is based upon *Me,* not upon the nature of your circumstances, which My love must *transform.*

Will you cultivate the daily making-sure that I am the focus of all that you most dearly desire?

I am a jealous God.

(Exodus 20.5)

My will is seen by so many as a barren thing, taking away from the potential of life, seen almost as something imposed by an enemy – to deprive humanity of a full existence. Many are led away from Me by such wrong assumptions.

My child, even for the dearest of My children there is normally a gulf between their own will and Mine . . . making imperfect the knowledge of Myself, as I really am. Understand that those areas in which our wills are *united* bring into play cosmic forces, and there is literally no limit to what can be achieved – even within the restrictions of a human existence. The wonderful truth is that newness of life is yours, for the choosing, moment by moment.

When you lovingly and humbly assent to My will, the Divine power is arrayed with you. You then become, during that period of harmony, a home where I *fully* dwell and against which nothing can prevail!

Walk in My sight . . . perfectly!
(Genesis 17.1)

Be careful to distinguish between *righteous* anger and indulgence in aggressive and harmful attitudes towards those who oppose you, or have little time for you.

Righteous anger must be directed against *evil*... the evil which can lie behind ways of those who trouble you. Seeing to the heart of the situation, you can recognise the activity of evil, which blinds, and which causes destruction, or self-destruction. Evil's threat is against *Me*; you can stand aside and not nurse the hurts as personal... merely evil's attempt to hold up your work for My cause.

It is right to feel outraged about all that opposes My kingdom of love and of peace, and which keeps My children from that for which I created them. To see the true cause of these things is to see others mis-using their free-will, but under a *definite pressure to do so*.

Show, towards others, the same generosity and patience, and understanding, which you have received from Me!

**Be merciful . . .
as your heavenly Father is merciful.**

(Luke 6.36)

*T*he world sees joy as something *received*... Many are trying to extract from life that which life may seem reluctant to give. So often, of course, this ends in disillusionment. *Enduring* happiness is only found on the narrow way with Me.

My joy may not be recognised as such by those who look elsewhere than to Me; it is inseparable from giving . . . found supremely in the joy which I Myself always experience in lending My resources to the often pitiful condition of My children; it is the joy which you experience in giving, not only to others – but to Me; it is the joy found in the inevitable humdrum tasks, when shared with Me.

Realise how profoundly I am comforted when room is made in a life for Me . . . Let this knowledge enable you to enter into the secret of all joy . . . simply the offering of what you have to your Lord – and to My children.

. . . sustained by doing the Father's will.

(John 4.34)

Remember to live with Me in 'the heavenly places' where there is no fear, nor hurry, nor fret of spirit.

I always honour your waiting upon Me; My thoughts are impressed upon you; all that I am must be *absorbed* by you. Waiting upon Me, you receive the assurance – which you must maintain – that all committed to Me is being surely worked out.

Yes, immerse yourself in Me – not looking anxiously within yourself to see what you are becoming! Keeping the sense of My presence, you can be alert to all that I am showing you.

Each 'working' day has its own restful influences, as you learn to receive My goodness through all that surrounds you. Remember that each time of prayer (however short), each look at the sky or at a tree, each thought of My love . . . all are restoring agencies . . . conveying My blessing. Enjoy Me, and My creation *in the midst of* duty-filled days.

Led beside water-springs.

(Isaiah 49.10)

My child, you rightly see that the past and the future are used by evil to distort the present.

Evil will attempt to make you 're-live' past incidents – particularly hurts where there was no reconciliation (and even, at times, when there *was* such reconciliation)! If you were hurt by someone who has since passed into My presence, remember that *truth* is now seen by that person; the particular blindness or unreasonableness on which you may be tempted to dwell, no longer exists. Evil, as always, has presented you with a lie.

In the same way, evil will paint lies concerning the future . . . leading you into needless apprehension, or, perhaps, the preparation of an unwise course. All that you have is the present. Enjoy the *serenity* of the present, which, for you, must always be filled with My love.

I am . . . Truth.

(John 14.6)

So often you will feel that I am forgetful about you, powerless to help you, or even that I am non-existent. Just as the material world at times, seems to deny the reality of My love, and of My spirit, so My apparent non-intervention would lead you to a wrong conclusion.

My child, irrespective of how you see your merit (or failure), irrespective of how you feel, always thank Me that I am answering your prayers… As you do this (whatever you may have in the way of 'evidence') My plans for you must be made perfect.

Learn utter dependence upon Me – not upon fluctuating moods, or even upon My revelations to you! At times when I seem remote, know that the strength and grace received for each day are *proof* of My constant companionship.

As you rely on Me, miracles are happening in you; although the miracle-work is often gradual, the time is of My ordaining, and is never wasted!

I will care for you to the end.

(Isaiah 46.4)

My love must *always* give you hope… hope born of conviction about Me; hope which no-one on earth can give to you. Hope placed, even tremblingly, in Me, becomes more than hope … There grows a sureness about the underlying *safety* of your existence … no matter how threatening passing events might be.

Hope without substance is a pitiable thing. But hope based on a permanent reality is wise . . . and is rewarded many times over.

Your future is being constantly, lovingly, prepared. I lift you from the entanglements of the material world to develop that true self for eternal life. Even in weakness, I take you forward … if *desire* is constant. I long – as you do – for our coming-together, one day . . . the goal of My love's plans for you.

Be sure of My *initiative* in creating the conditions for that meeting, (with no impediments), in the realm of My love.

In My Father's house are many dwelling-places.

(John 14.2)

Never let life's disappointments, and My seeming lack of response to specific prayers, cause you to doubt My *absolute* sufficiency.

You must have in your mind, *simultaneously*, the realism that many situations do not immediately change, and the trust that I can fulfil any purpose of Mine with sureness. I do not look on at your earthly conflicts dispassionately; I will an end to them, and only permit their continuance, as I have told you, because I can see ultimate blessing for you in them, however hard this may be to accept now.

My child, just *know* that anything in your life which I see as right to bring about. I *can* bring about. Never listen to the lie that apparent non-intervention means powerlessness. I am *ceaselessly* at work for you ... there need be no ruffling of the spirit. Remember that trust in My power to change situations . . . a trust which you will know has not been made in vain.

Your fears are groundless.

I am Alpha and Omega – the First and the Last.

(Revelation 22.13)

To grieve over failures leads to the removal of impediments in our relationship; but to *remain* self-accused (doubting My promises of healing and restoration) gratifies the wish of evil, affecting your enjoyment of My promises. Do not take upon yourself *My* role . . . judging yourself, and therefore living in fear. Let My love reach those deep source-areas, where you may be almost permanently self-condemned.

Guilt will always spell danger; guilt can produce yet more that is wrong! If your passionate aim is to please Me, know that oppressive guilt is never of Myself. Nowhere is trust in My promises more important than in the realm of forgiveness.

When evil masquerades as the punishing guardian of obedience, stand with Me against it; let Me silence all other voices but the voice of welcoming love, if *My* will is your desire.

I uplift the penitent ones.

(Isaiah 57.15)

My child, do not be afraid, to be 'invaded' . . . seen in your human weakness, but with a definite trust in Me. Do not feel that this vulnerability will deter others; rather, it will wonderfully speak of My power to uphold one human life . . . yours!

It is in weakness, and in an atmosphere of *truth* rather than spiritual posturing, that I can be seen.

At times you will be rewarded by others' recognition of Myself in you . . . quite irrespective of your emotions and your pre-occupations. For your encouragement, I will permit others to speak of that recognition – and of your help to them. This is your proof that an offer to be My servant is always taken up and acted upon!

Your small part is to ignore variable feelings and remain focussed upon Me – ready for all that I desire, so very much, to give you.

I am glorified in them.
(John 17.10)

Laying-up treasure in heaven is a *continuing process* as you value, most highly, the things of the Spirit.

> Every prayer said, lovingly, . . .
> Every thoughtful act, . . .
> Every conquest over self, . . .
> Every self-deprivation of life's shallower things, in order to make room for Me . . .
> all are building up an inheritance for you.

It is not that the good you do on earth 'earns' that inheritance . . . it could not! It is simply that a law is being kept . . . a law by which everything prompted by Myself upon which you act, has an inevitable consequence. The treasure which awaits you is one which you may not recognise now, but which is kept for all who trust Me.

My child, value – desperately – all that is of truth and light and sacrificial love. Make your inheritance secure . . . and let My other children be led to desire to share it with you!

Come, you who are blessed of My Father.

(Matthew 25.34)

I go ahead of you into life's bewildering, and often frightening, places.

How foolish it is to be apprehensive about what the future holds.

> Into those occasions which you dread
> I have gone... to prepare a way for
> My trusting child.

> Into those occasions still beyond your
> anticipation I have gone . . . to make
> them fit into My purpose for you.

Transcending time, I can be so close to you *now*, and yet influence that which still awaits you. My child, is your trust still utterly in Myself as your guide? Rejoice if this is so, because you are among the few who have found the narrow way which leads to life . . . You can journey with even more courage . . . and even more joy!

I will receive you.

(John 14.3)

The certainty of life's destination, if that life is shared with Me, will wonderfully uplift you every day. The thought of what awaits My followers has a power to sustain and to encourage... which is possessed by no earthly agency.

What may have seemed merely a fond wish is transformed into a certainty by the daily communion with Myself.

Remember that I was in the world, essentially, to draw alongside you in it, and to lead you through it to that destination of which I have spoken often.

Do not speculate about the content of life beyond your present one; merely accept such continuation as a *fact,* and be content that the place to which you are led is a place filled with My love.

My child, look up from the road, with its pitfalls, and see the welcoming light at its end . . . your destination is . . . *Myself.*

If it were not so, I would have told you.

(John 14.2)

Life's many hazards arise from a developing creation, and there are spiritual hazards, as you have found. Even towards those who do not acknowledge Me there is, (because of My love), an attitude of protection. That protection, however, can never be as all-embracing as when I am, consciously, brought into a life as its main hope.

Thank Me that I continue to shield you from influences which would cause great havoc in your mental processes, and eventually destroy your life. Humanity's protective instincts are imperfect; *My* protection is constant, indivisible from My love, not something to be 'called upon' or, perhaps, withdrawn.

Will you see not My power but, rather, My love, as the shielding agent? In times of great stress see My love as both shielding and healing that which was wounded.

Are you beginning to see how many-sided is the activity of My love?

**My sheep shall go in and out,
and find pasture.**

(John 10.9)

Clinging to My promises can change, miraculously, even the most fearful life!

Behind each promise see My all-enveloping love, which strikes at the roots of fear . . . man's ultimate fear being that of extinction. As a promise is warmly received, fear is replaced by a peace, a hope, and a courage which can withstand misfortunes and seeming disadvantages.

The promises are so that you should never despair . . . stand upon them when afraid and let the *presence* contained in the promise help you. My promises are given to those who, conscious of being weak and variable, are single-minded about the one thing which matters . . . following Me.

Man cannot see that where a life is based on a divine promise, circumstances are robbed of their fear-capacity. *All* My promises will be fulfilled and evil-based fears exposed as having no foundation. My child, a promise anchored in your heart means that you will never be overwhelmed.

**I tell you these things so that,
when they happen, you might believe.**

(John 14.29)

I know that what I say to you in My word is of great comfort, and of great encouragement to you. This is unfailing. Will you also try to see that My word goes *beyond* these things . . . ensuring that the sense of being temporarily uplifted does not end there?

Will you try to ensure that the greater love kindled in you when waiting upon Me, is translated into the often exacting encounters of life?

My word is not in order that there should be momentary experience of the heavenly dimension! It is in order that the whole complexion of your life should take on that dimension. My word is given so that joy, self-control, the eye of love, utter tranquillity, should be so much part of you, that you take them for granted. My child, ensure the *continuity* of My word . . . into the framework of your day-to-day life.

Not everyone saying "Lord, Lord"
will enter the Kingdom,
but those obeying My Father's will.

(Matthew 7.21)

The sense of continuity is one of the priceless gifts of life shared with Me.

You have found the great blessing, and the great stability for your character, of My unchanging presence, in a bewildering succession of circumstances. This may not be fully appreciated until, perhaps, a sense of that presence is temporarily lost, during a painful period of doubt.

Life can rob you, in a moment, of every familiar support, and of all your sources of being sustained. You then look for any fixed point, anything resembling what once sustained you. You look in vain until it dawns upon you that there I am . . . still loving, still guarding you.

How much the world loses in a sense of identity and of stability if I am not there at every turn of the road . . . you know that the closer you are to Me the safer will be your walk!

I do not change!

(Malachi 3.6)

My child, everything which I allow in your life is something for which you can thank Me. You are blest to know this . . . only My Spirit can reveal it to you. You can take full advantage of the *opportunities* in each situation.

Upon your past, present and future My wisdom is brought to bear . . . a wisdom springing from My concern for you. To find your joy in Me in all situations must be learned *quickly*. At times of great uncertainty be *especially* sure of My activity for you. You can, therefore, go on thanking Me all the time . . . Let the world see in you the patience and cheerfulness of the heart which looks to Me for everything; let it see what My victory over evil has achieved.

All the things after which men strive are not worthy to be set beside possessing *Me*.

I am your great reward.

(Genesis 15.1)

My child, I am saddened that the world still does not recognise the full significance of My involving Myself, to the limit, in human experience. There are many pointers in My creation to the fact of Myself, but none are conclusive. When I entered the pattern of history it was so that this should be the one point of certainty, not only for that generation, but for all My children since.

All *genuine* knowledge of the divine, whatever its outward form, is a response to that revelation of God among men, although partial knowledge is not withheld from other areas of human experience.

Certainty was wonderfully awakened in those who saw the divine in an earthly setting, but that is not all . . . Certainty, rather than mystery, is possible for *all* who live outside the time of that revelation. This happens when that event is deliberately, and with a sense of wonder, locked away in one's heart.

I will draw all men to Myself.

(John 12.32)

My child, never be so overwhelmed by life's reverses that you fail to reach out, *immediately,* to Me.

Disappointments, great sorrows, can be made so much worse – seemingly beyond help – if the instinctive reaching-out is forgotten. Be so attuned to My presence that *every* experience is shared with Me, reaching out before bitterness or despair become established.

Learn to see My love enfolding every hurt; in *some* way My love is bringing about that which one day you will see as a cause for thanksgiving. Anything other than peace is not My will for you! Refuse to wander from that known way, moving, firmly, towards the wonderful things which I have planned for you.

Because you are surrendered to Me, I share all your experiences. My victory is absolute, and you can be sure of heading towards fulfilment of all your spiritual ambitions. My child, I thank you for your growing love towards Me.

I revive the spirits of the humble.

(Isaiah 57.15)

Conflict and effort only mean that there is *life* within. My Spirit taking you forward! Seeking to follow My commands, you are at the place on the road that *I* wish you to be; this represents *real* progress, no matter what you, or others, may judge.

It is part of evil's strategy to induce discouragement, seeing in your failures a falling back in your spiritual life, blinded to your victories achieved with Me. Is your confidence still in Me? Then be *equally* sure that these are times of great gain.

My child, doubt of your progress is doubt of Me. Even a little progress shows My purposes being fulfilled. You are learning life's lessons and finding that, with Me, it is a winning struggle. You will enjoy a new quality of life as you believe in all that I have done in you. All that you need for a new life is *already yours*.

**It will not be by mere strength,
but by My spirit.**

(Zechariah 4.6)

My child, relationships are not spoiled until *both* say or do that which brings in a more permanent factor. While *you* show restraint and rely on Me, the possibility of change comes from *your own very restraint* and reflection of Me! The hurt is then more quickly dissolved.

I can only create love and harmony where I am *allowed* to do so . . . as you avoid the blockages of fruitless recrimination, controversy, and intrusion of the 'hurt' self, as you pray, and let Me work upon the situation.

You have learned that the way of love can be hard . . . but never as hard as when you *depart* from that way! The power of My love, when *permitted* to work, is the great binder-up of misunderstandings and even of deep hatreds. Alas, the world (because of its indifference to Me), has yet to experience just how much the influence of My love can achieve.

Pray for those who ill-treat you.

(Matthew 5.44)

To be unwavering in your trust in My word, think of its Giver . . . in whose hands your life has been securely led. Embrace that word, for it affects every part of your life, knowing that My nature, and the truth which I have made known, are unchanging. Ponder My word much more!

To every heart not closed by pride or by self-will, My word, with all its promises, is presented. Where I see the spirit of acceptance, I make it possible for the wealth promised to be claimed.

Because this existence has a *soul*, My word is a living word to which you come, eager to be fed. My word brings you immediately into the divine realm of peace and patience.

If My word lives in you and is expressed in your way of life, there is that strongest possible identification of My victorious being with your own.

My word accomplishes My purposes.

(Isaiah 55.11)

At the heart of all existence is a natural law . . . under this law, love and endurance simply attract to themselves the Divine rewards. Although My rewards may appear to be delayed by the world's limitations, they are *sure*, and, when realised, their duration is infinite.

Never feel that acts of kindness, or of loving restraint, are ever wasted . . . they have attracted to themselves something of eternity!

You now realise, My child, that the essential reward is *Myself.* Having won Me, the result will be un-thought of bliss and enlightenment. There is always a foretaste, in the present, of that which awaits you; this does not take you out of the present, or make the present unreal . . it *enriches* the present.

I have decreed an eventual end to human sorrow. Sorrow will indeed turn into an enduring joy. Frequently, lift up your heart to Me – expressing the trust which has been growing, steadily, in you. Remember that your destination is fixed.

Well done, good and faithful servant!

(Matthew 25.21)

Life's gifts, helping to make endurable an often-painful road, can all be traced to *Myself*.

My children who do not know Me find satisfactions which do not contain the essential element of Myself . . . satisfactions which prove transitory, and eventually add yet more burdens to the darker side of life.

What is of Me, all around you, is limitless, if only it is *recognised*.

Apart from all that is uplifting in nature itself, there is the deep satisfaction of human friendship and devotion – given and received – the wonderful peace when long-standing relationships are healed after forgiveness, all innocent laughter, all tasks which bring a sense of purpose and achievement. There is so much that I can share with you because I am *already part* of that experience . . . its origin!

My joy in them.

(John 17.13)

To witness for Me is essentially very simple; it is beyond eloquence and beyond persuasion. The world will quickly recognise your sense of *gratitude* at being rescued from futility and constant failures; it will, of course, quickly recognise My love in you!

All these things – culminating in your overwhelming thankfulness to Me – will speak to the hearts of others . . . they will recognise the *presence* of One who gave all, to offer men hope once again. Your newness of life and My using you are one natural whole.

Those living without Me will readily detect your indebtedness to Me, and will be ready (even if hesitatingly at first), to find what I can do for *them*.

Let your simple *words* tell of Me, as I give you the opportunity. Let, also, what is *unspoken* (your love and thankful heart towards Me), bring glory to My name.

Go to your friends and tell them what the Lord has done for you.

(Mark 5.19)

141

My child, ascend, with Me, the steps which lead to the place of glory . . . steps fashioned from the stony places which you encounter – steps upon which I create a place of victory for you.

Ensure that the process of ascending is a continuing one.

> Where courage has been gained, *use* it.
> Where wisdom has been gained, *use* it.

My child, *consolidation* is so important on your pilgrimage, the dark places providing wonderful opportunities. Great things are done in you as you come through these places with Me.

Cling to your gains … look for infinitely *more*… rather than fearing to lose what you have! Realise how *much* you are losing whenever you stand still, or needlessly surrender victories, in the essentially *upward* calling of being My chosen one.

**In heaven is kept a treasure
which will not fail you.**

(Luke 12.33)

It will make all the difference – especially in those sudden crises – if you have learned to see Me accompanying you, supporting you . . . My *light* around you on the road!

Sometimes the effort of another step will seem impossible; you will shrink from what lies ahead of you. At those times, make it a rule to affirm that I am there with you. *Look* into the glorious sufficiency of My presence. Let your Companion lift you forward . . . not letting you go for one instant! When courage fails, and you feel impelled to act defeatedly, turn to love's light and go forward.

The realisation of your spiritual hopes would, of course, be impossible without Me. *With* Me, you can feel the exhilaration of rising above obstacles and all earth's disappointments. Journey with Me . . . along the way known *only* to Me.

I am with you . . . always.

(Matthew 28.20)

My child, so much is offered . . . and so much is unused! What is offered is so much more than a pattern to achieve; many have been discouraged by this inadequate concept of life with Me. It is sad that sharing My life is presented in a barren way, without showing the wealth which would make one anxious to possess it.

The supreme gift offered is that of being able to feed upon the Divine love . . . All the soul-qualities needed for that continuing life with Me are granted as I am taken into a life. Each day is a unique opportunity to live usefully and joyfully.

I Myself am the embodiment of all the things of hope presented to this world. Be free from burdens of the spirit, free to have true concern for others, to carry out My law of love.

My child, you are fortunate in your knowledge of Me, through My word to you!

**When he found one precious pearl,
he sold everything in order to buy it.**

(Matthew 13.46)

You will have learned that you can be serene when there is so much to do, and that you can be fretful and burdened when there are few calls upon you! All depends upon the degree of harmony with Myself. Be faithful in the important things – with no 'fussiness' beyond what is reasonable . . . just your clear duty of the moment.

I make Myself dependent upon your faith and upon your concern for others at the human level. Even when much is uncertain or threatening, know that you are much used – because of My moulding of you. As you give to others, I *recharge* you . . . which is why you experience a sense of refreshment after I have met someone's need through you.

Let Me develop in you the gift of *uplifting* others – simply by your presence. Cultivate the *will* to show love . . . even at times when your own heart may be breaking.

You are My servant and will bring glory to My Name.

(Isaiah 49.3)

Try to both *give* more and to *receive* more!

Launch out in the knowledge that many will receive Me through yourself. Consciously resting in My love, you can be a source of joy, re-assurance and peace to those around you. It is *My* love with which you will love others; it is this same love which returns to Me from your own heart!

Be sure that every contact is helpful and positive; the *quantity* is not the important thing. There is danger if too much is attempted, and what is done for Me becomes grim and burdensome; this is why receiving is so important . . .

Times of taking life's good things (as from Me), times of praising Me and delighting in Me, are as pleasing to Me as your service. Yes, fill your life with both giving and receiving . . . with fear cast out.

I will make you bright for the world to see.

(Isaiah 49.6)

$\mathcal{A}$ mood of optimism can quickly crumble if the world is all that one has! Realism – especially as the years pass – causes dread to so many, or the resignation that past happiness may never recur.

My child, it is the sense of future which gives the element of thrill to a growing relationship with Myself . . . Even with the passing years, every interest, every ambition can still be a cause for enthusiasm.

This, to the unbeliever, may seem illogical, but where a life has Me as its foundation, there is an awareness that whatever worthwhile is undertaken, carries with it a sense of permanence.

The amount of time left in a life does not matter… because whatever is begun, at any stage, will be seen as part of a continuing process.

The Lord God will be your everlasting light.
(Isaiah 60.19)

All that is of Me is of the realm of light... the light of My Person, by which you see, more readily, the world's deceptions, its lures, its superficiality, its vain self-sufficiency. By that light you see My love unfolding in many hearts; you see the patient working-out of the creative process; you see the qualities of the soul (never to be extinguished), in so many of My children.

My child, darkness beguiles with false promises, ready to take you from My path... but the light is always there as you resolutely turn to it, the light of My love for you.

Let My light shine upon sudden or predicted challenges. To change the 'tone' of each circumstance let My love's light shine upon it. Exclude what is of darkness by that unwavering gaze towards light's source . . . your Friend who is so close to you.

Believe in the light!

(John 12.35)

It is only when you come to realise, deeply, My responsibility for you that you begin to lose pre-occupation, in various ways, with self. So much of your mind's energy can be poured into pursuit of objectives which have self at the heart of them, energy flowing into fretfulness about material needs, and even about what you may or may not be achieving for Me!

Dis-entangle yourself from vain efforts which are concerned with provision of personal needs, with establishing status, with the securing of results.

Vital changes occur as you reflect upon My moment-by-moment responsibility for you. You will experience a great release . . . permitting My influence to work in ways which are infinitely more effective. Peace will live in you and love will flow from you . . . No longer intermittently !

**The birds, who do not sow, are fed
by your heavenly Father.**

(Matthew 6.26)

My child, I want you to exercise your wisdom, endowed by Me. You fail Me whenever you listen to other voices. Your own wisdom's influence upon the course of your life, and upon that of others around you, must be fully permitted, as you keep close to Me.

Where there is genuine uncertainty, I want you, more than ever, to bank upon the divine wisdom. I cannot err. The strands of your life are fashioned by My wisdom into what is compatible with your eternal destiny.

In confusing places, look away to My wisdom, so that you may know peace; your look is telling Me of your belief that I know, precisely, the course which your life must take, and precisely the times of My perfect intervention for you.

Nothing which violates the divine wisdom will, in the long term, remain in your circumstances where there is, in you, an attitude of trust and acceptance.

The Holy Spirit will receive what is of Me and show it to you.

(John 16.14)

My child, you may often find yourself using the name "wonderful" when addressing Me… said with a growing freedom, and with a growing conviction.

This is true praise . . . not necessarily in the eyes of man, but expressing the amazement of your own heart at all that I have done for you – and what you realise I can *be* for you.

"Wonderful" is the attempt to express that which has left men speechless . . . the love and provision, and sense of safety which have been found in trusting Me. Your saying of the word to Me tells Me that you are joining with those, through the ages, who have felt precisely that, concerning Myself.

Saying it to Me acts as a confirmation in your own heart (often to be drawn upon in time of trouble), that you have made the wisest choice which it is possible to make!

With whom will you compare Me?

(Isaiah 40.25)

Never under-estimate the *power* released by your prayers – even those said wistfully more than confidently! This will always help you to show patience.

Approach *all* your duties prayerfully and unhurriedly, ensuring that My influence surrounds them; this will mean a poise in your life, as you become aware of our *partnership.*

Learn the direct link between power and patience. There is a disharmony in My using of you if you wish to see, or to force, the desired outcome of your efforts. When I counsel you to be 'relaxed and trusting' this *always* involves prayer; My love dominant; inviting *Me* into every problem.

Remind yourself, frequently, of the *constant* Divine activity which accompanies your worship of Me, your surrender to Me. Truly, without Me you can do nothing.

Ask – and it will be given to you.

(Matthew 7.7)

You can see, in the ingenuity and achievements of mankind, the use of what I bestowed upon human nature . . . inventiveness, sound judgement, far-sightedness, and the use of knowledge for the advancement of others.

Only those who share life with Me are *also* aware of the constant attempts by evil to frustrate the hopes and dreams and strivings of men.

So much which could bring blessing to My world is diverted from its goal. So much that would benefit mankind can be tragically spoiled if evil's influence is *not recognised.*

Only partnership with Myself can guard against the spoilation of life's good designs. Only partnership with Me can *reverse* this process... and build wonderful things from the apparent failures of earth!

The Prince of this world will be overthrown.

(John 12.31)

Learn to rest your spirit *just where you are.* So often you cannot be where there is freedom from recurring demands. But you *can* find immediate rest of spirit, with Me, in any environment. Turn to the Friend who is *already there* with you, anxious to impart a precious sense of stillness, which other agencies could not achieve.

My child, you know that I and My Father are one . . . It is this loving *Fatherhood* to which you come, and let all your cares go from you.

How much My world needs those who are rested in spirit, and can carry My influence into life's complexities and its foolishness. Rested in Spirit… showing itself in the attributes by which the world will know that, truly, you are My disciple. Yes, rest in Me and *give* to Me your love, your trust, all that is in you.

You who are thirsty . . . come and drink!

(Isaiah 55.1)

To come to My word *always* means a new situation. A change is made in you whenever the power of My word is allowed its full course.

You must never forget the resource to which you have immediate access even when, in a place of darkness, there is either doubt of Me, or a temporary disinclination to seek Me. The ambition of evil is consistent: to drive a wedge between us. Evil knows that whenever I am allowed, as now, to speak by My Spirit, the change-element beginning in you will eventually transform, radically, the situation in which you are placed. Keep your hope alive by thanking Me that I can do all things.

The presence of My word in you guarantees an influence upon everything which involves others in your life.

To feed upon My word is never more necessary than when temptation to spiritual discouragement is strong.

**Hearing the Word,
receiving it, and producing much fruit.**

(Mark 4.20)

Only a true child of Mine can know the *loneliness* of following Me.

At times, My calling seems to isolate even from those dearest to you, and who want only your happiness. Seeking My will will provoke frequent misunderstandings; there will be painful choices between following My way and another way (harmless on the surface) which is pleasing to those near you.

Only a true child of Mine can enter into My loneliness when seen upon earth. But that is not all.

Loneliness and misunderstanding served only to *enhance* My consciousness of the Father's presence. In loneliness, I will be radiating, in *your* life, the quiet hope which speaks clearly of My presence with you. I will be glorified in your life, increasingly.

**It is your Father's good pleasure
to give you the Kingdom.**

(Luke 12.32)

The presence, in you, of My Spirit, means that in your life is enacted something of the universal conflict present in My creation. When conflict is fierce, when the walk of peace and joy is challenged, recognise the perpetual challenge of evil to My cause.

Instead of being cast down, of stoically accepting a way of failure as inevitable, glance up to the victorious Lord, against whom the challenge of evil is bound to fail.

As you trustingly *use* what I have given you, evil is powerless against you . . . think of your *impregnability!*

See the ultimate victory, in creation, of My cause as that which is possible in your own life. This will help you to see all that is of darkness as *conquerable* – and destined, in you, to be put to flight . . . just as surely as it will within My universe.

The glory given to Me, I have given to them!

(John 17.22)

My child, ask for the grace which you need to choose My way. You then become caught up in the *cycle* of My grace:

> Grace assisting you to make the right choices; Your own conscious effort and determination; Grace completing and fulfilling.

To be more and more lost in Me can involve sacrifice – but remember that the way to My Kingdom is straight. There must be a *resolution*, fired by the thought of My love and of My victory, that old ways must go; I leave no vacuum! You have all that you need for change. You are being led towards knowing Me with increasing clarity.

The end is assured . . . but I want you to enter the stage of victory *now* . . . a victory always bringing the *peace* of conquest.

**Happy are those
who are hungry and thirsty for goodness.**

(Matthew 5.6)

My child, I have told you never to doubt My mercy. Forgiveness pours out from Me because My purposes are essentially forward.

My love consigns sin, repented over, to the place where it must never, for a moment, hinder either My purposes, or yours. I see your remorse *only* as removing temporary barriers between us, and as restoring you.

All that I am concerned about is your learning the lessons of failure and inadequate trust, and then looking with Me to the *future* . . . all that matters.

Your regrets, your bitterness, your self-pity, your disappointment with yourself, must be consigned to the past, rather than allowed to exist in the present. Think, instead, of how tiny is the stretch of time in which life's imperfections exist; compare that stretch of time with the eternity in which you will develop, within My love, the essential you – the soul infinitely precious to Me.

I will forgive their wrong-doing and forget it completely.

(Jeremiah 31.34)

Human nature is disinclined to allow My light fully to penetrate areas of darkness within.

As you cling to ways which are manifestations of the old unsaved self, the light which would speak to the world of My possession of you is obscured. To allow light's entrance may, at times, be painful – the unsaved self is reluctant to surrender that in which it has mistakenly found security.

Make it habitual, firstly, to gaze, without fear – and eagerly – into My light. Then submit, fully, to the enlightening process – seeing what desperately needs to be eliminated, so that the divine light prevails in you. Allow Me to lighten *your entire life.*

My child, never be afraid to cast off ways which you use as spurious sources of support; instead let My sustaining presence bear you.

If your right hand offends, cut it off.

(Matthew 5.30)

You must see the *true* nature of joy.

Do not feel that you must seek the excitement, only temporarily existing, which is tied to gratification of the senses, or to the realisation of some earthly plan. These things are *snares* for you.

My command that joy must exist in you means that *all* that is of Me, from whatever source, becomes the food of the spirit.

The quality of joy found in Me – and, of course, in expressing Me – has permanence.

Where there is hope, where there is self-forgetfulness, where concern for others takes over from self, joy need not be longed for; it has become part of you!

Your heart will find happiness!

(John 16.22)

My child, grasp the *unlimited* nature of what I have in store for you . . . as unlimited as is My love. As you look at your present pattern of life, the environment in which you try to trust My word, do not feel that My promises are unreal, or in conflict with reason. In *your* hands lies the early fulfilment of those promises.

All that I have given you to hope for has been in the sure knowledge of the Divine working. Hope, for you, lies in My bringing the complex strands of life into an area of order and completion. Although you may reflect, frequently, upon your own weakness, I want you also to be filled with love and gratitude that *all* that I have promised to My children will be realised.

Your new way of living will show that you are trusting the hope given to you; it will show that you are not listening to the voice of doubt (based on your past failure-experience), but to the voice of truth. Has the wonderful truth about that new way *really* dawned upon you? Remember My word that everything which I have asked of you is within your grasp!

I will satisfy My people with My goodness.

(Jeremiah 31.14)

$\mathcal{A}$re you applying My often-repeated injunction to allow Me to work?

How many imperfect designs, destined to failure, can occur when My influence is restricted. My influence is restricted by the basic belief that such influence is not being exerted!

How often must I tell you that My love for you has imposed upon Me the obligation to steer you through life's complexities in a way which is for your greatest good?

Pause, frequently, to ask yourself, in the midst of pressing demands, whether I am being given that *freedom* to assist you; ask whether you are trusting the power of your prayers on your own and others' behalf.

The more your life reflects My sureness, the more perfect will be the designs which begin with you.

My Father goes on working, and so do I.

(John 5.17)

When someone has been hurt, and the blame directed towards yourself, you will have found that there is so little which can be done immediately . . . persuasion or anger may seem only to make matters worse.

In My intimate knowledge of the factors involved you must bring it to Me immediately. As a duty, ask for forgiveness for anything which I see to have been wrong or causative on your part. With absolute confidence, give the heart of the person or persons to Me . . . trusting the victory of My good influence over evil whenever prayer is made.

Give the circumstances to Me, so that I may bring good out of them. Thank Me that I am doing so! Let Me keep out disturbed feelings and the pressure to 'put things right' in your way. Let My love and approval feed your spirit.

Be ready for My prompting about what you can do, with wisdom and grace, knowing that, already, My influence has been upon those concerned . . . including yourself!

I will hear your prayers.

(Jeremiah 29.12)

It is only when embarking, in earnest, on life's walk with Me that you realise the imperative of keeping very closely to what I have described as My narrow way.

You realise what the narrow way is *not*: it is not a way of restriction, for its own sake. The unease which you experience when departing, momentarily, from that way has shown you that any departure opens the door to a havoc-making incursion by evil.

Therefore you see what the narrow way *is:* it is the way in which our *unity* remains fully intact, with all the power taken into you as a consequence. It is the way of service and of restfulness.

Your earnest desire to remain on My way means that there will always be a warning voice, giving you the opportunity to avoid danger.

The way leading to destruction is wide.

(Matthew 7.13)

Many have gone astray from Me in the name of 'religion'. My child, I want your desire for Me to have that almost-desperate quality, your trust in My word to have that same quality, your reverence for My person to contain no compromise.

Within My church, sadly, there are many inducements – inspired by evil – to be content with a comfortable scepticism, to live by worldly standards.

Within My Body, you are *needed* by My other children; here, you will receive from others whose lives are centred upon Me. Maintain that extravagant, worshipping attitude towards Myself – let it be shared with others.

Let there be no half-measures. You can be sure that My Body of believers will be strengthened more than you can imagine by your zeal for Me, in the place where you are.

Be lost in love, and worship, and trust!

What do you truly think of Christ?
(Matthew 22.42)

My child, it is vital to attend to *actions*.

Never feel that newness of life is impossible for you because you are led, from time to time, into dark, resentful, unloving thoughts. Because evil's pressure is constant, such thoughts are bound to occur; you must resolutely refuse to be identified with them, and turn from them immediately.

Refuse to be committed to any *action* affecting others – words or deeds which I give you the instinctive ability to recognise, and to turn aside from, in My strength. This will become second nature to you.

Yes, My child, it is possible, in spite of conflicts within, to turn away, joyfully, from any outward *commitment* to things not of My Spirit.

Fight and win . . . for My love's sake.

Go away, Satan!
(Matthew 4.10)

My child, remember that My love is unaffected by your failures and shortcomings. You have seen how this principle operates where there is love at the human level. At the human level, however, patience can eventually run out, and love die.

It is important for you to keep in mind the *constancy* of My love . . . not in order to make light of wrong in your life, but so that you will never, in any circumstances, feel that you are held back from communion with Me. See all the divine promises of mercy summed up in Me. It is because your responsive trust, and the inter-action of our spirits, means so much to Me that love's constancy can be depended upon.

Let My love burn into you at progressively deeper levels . . . bringing, firstly, decreasing hurt to Myself; and, secondly, an understanding towards those around you which, (in a small way), reflects My own towards you!

He ran out and embraced him.

(Luke 15.20)

Even in sorrow, My world must be seen as one which can *give* to you.

Those agencies of beauty, with power to uplift, are not robbed of their power when life becomes shadowed.

As you allow My love to heal the spirit in life's almost unbearable misfortunes, allow it, also, to reach you through the untarnished aspects of My creation.

Let nature's beauty mingle with dejection within; let many things which you may have enjoyed when life was relatively good *still* play their part in conveying My strengthening presence.

Let nature's beauty, and all its gifts, speak to you the eternal message of hope . . . the life which is to be enjoyed with Me when present darkness has passed.

**I will create a pathway in the wilderness
and rivers in the desert.**

(Isaiah 43.19)

You will change a life of wanting into a life of achieving . . . as you develop that sheer dependency upon Me. I foresaw this change at the moment when your heart was illuminated with the conviction that I was the only answer for your need.

I came into your heart because, in spite of inevitable areas of rebellion, I saw growing consciousness of need, your recognition that I could supply it. I foresaw your earnest seeking... and your eventual relationship with Myself; I had to break the element of self-will so that you would allow Me to shape your life's circumstances.

The plan for your life, as you well know, is carried out in My strength. *Joyful* resignation to My will is the basis for real spiritual progress . . . and for those intimations of My presence which are bound to follow. Rejoice that My choosing you was in foreknowledge of your eventually reaching the place made ready for you in My Kingdom.

**I have drawn you to Myself
with loving kindness.**

(Jeremiah 31.3)

If you have never felt an ache in your spirit, an inward tear, then you have not entered into My own consciousness of life's pain.

The world has its own often-harsh descriptions for the sad-at-heart, but wistfulness and sorrow are *natural* in your perception of what life could be, and what it is, in reality.

Sharing My existence does not mean a brittle optimism, one lacking in sensitivity; it means weeping with Me over My world.

Such sadness finds a place alongside the times of joy and hope which inevitably accompany your recognition of My working in your life.

Sorrow has filled your heart.

(John 16.6)

My child, *use* Me . . . Use me in conquering all that would spoil a life (in My love), of peace, trust, gladness, and really blest service for Me.

Because you are no longer under the compulsion to indulge in the old ways; they can now be replaced by Spirit-filled living. Let Me show you wrong ways remaining, so that you may gently surrender them . . . the submission of one who knows that love plans what is best for you. Let impediments be ruthlessly and systematically dealt with.

My purposes cannot be frustrated, but can be held up by continued disobedience, and by doubting Me when confidence in Me was perfectly possible for you! I am able to interpret My will effectively in *every* human situation involving yourself.

**God is pruning you
to make you even more fruitful.**

(John 15.2)

Many feel that leaving Me out of life is avoiding mystery and silence and enjoying life's certainties.

Those who are content to live without Me fail to see that although I cannot be superficially discerned, I am wonderfully met in that silence, and in that apparent 'non-activity'.

My child, never be tempted to take your life's mood, on any day, from periodic feelings that I am remote or unwilling to intervene. Instead, remember, warmly, the countless occasions when My presence has consoled you, has brought relief, has caused you to hope again. I still *anticipate* every possible need.

In the so-called 'stillness' of My working you find countless occasions of overflowing with thankfulness!

Just rest your spirit in all that you see in Me.

You refuse to come to me to find true life!

(John 5.40)

Evil would want you to believe that I hold back from supplying your need – because you may have surrendered your right to fullness of supply.

Be sure that your falls, your occasions of hurting Me, have *not* affected My desire for you to have the very best planned for you – now and in the future. My grace becomes a stepping-stone to a greater closeness to, and appreciation of, Myself.

The hands of supply are outstretched still . . . receive!

From Me receive peace, receive courage, with nothing held back. The love which I have for you can never be checked in its out-pouring.

Let there be many occasions when, with sins forgiven, you open up yourself, and simply receive love's bounty. You realise that the implications of My love are limitless.

The Bread of God gives life to the world.

(John 6.32)

Never let tangible 'success' be the end of your striving after holiness. In serving Me you must not be concerned with results, in a calculating way. Self-will (even in ambition for My cause) must be eliminated. Love to serve Me in the way which I see is the best possible, your energies applied for Me, not for subtle self-advancement in My service.

Follow the *prayerful* ways of service, desiring *My* glory. Your agency has always to be according to My purposes. As you look to Me in surrender, I can flow through you at *My* choosing.

My child, ask to see things with My eye, increasingly. Ask that your will may be in more perfect alignment with Mine . This is always *your* main work. Never lose sight of it!

My thoughts are not your thoughts!

(Isaiah 55.8)

This is a world in which the operation of My power is wilfully restricted by man. My influence is excluded by man's desire to be in control of his own destiny, to live to his own standards.

My child, although this is not so in your life, see the danger of restricting the operation of My power . . . occurring when you feverishly plan what would have been so much better left to Myself. All that I can then do is to continue to care for you, but watch you hold up those very factors which would answer your prayers.

Eventually, My plans for you *must* be accomplished, but so much frustration, so much bitter regret occurs when self-will, rather than trust, motivates you . . . even if only for some of the time. My child, show the restraint which speaks of My greatness. Evil wishes you to curtail the flow of My power on your behalf. Ensure that I can bring about, *without* imperfection, My loving purposes for you.

Do not be complacent in your wisdom.

(Jeremiah 9.23)

It is *only* with Me – your life's goal fixed – that you can notice the fashioning of steps towards Myself out of what would seem utterly pointless and barren. Those who do not know Me cannot see My ordaining of the world as the way of the soul's fulfilment. You will see it increasingly.

Although the world may not see your purposeful walk with Me, you will know, in your heart, a vital *new direction* to your life; following that direction, you will never be overwhelmed.

Giving all into My sure hands, your present and future . . . a *fresh* giving every day . . . ensures My continuing activity. Always see Me as not merely in control of the creative process, but in control of your life . . . The abandonment of pride, and self-sufficiency, will then bring about great things in one very imperfect, but willing, child!

Rejoice in what I am bringing about.

(Isaiah 65.18)

The nature of the Divine love is not always understood. It is a *longing* love . . . often painfully drawing My children towards Me. My love is constantly hurt, but inexorably, breaks down resistance; it does not tire, as does human love.

My child, see the patient activity of My love – especially in your own heart . . . taking away all that has offended against itself.

My love must *fill* you. The self-seeking, the calculated ends, which contaminate your own imperfect love, must disappear. *My* wishes rather than expediency!

Recognise My love's growth in your own resolve to break down all barriers, all misunderstandings. When your love is hurt, recognise the affinity with My own. Your love, blending with Mine, will be greatly used in My purposes for My world.

. . . so that I, too, may be in them.

(John 17.26)

It is because love is the mainspring of all phenomena that it is always challenged by evil. When *love* can be destroyed, evil is satisfied – much more than with more obvious and superficial temptations.

The collapse of love is always life's foremost tragedy; it means that everything planned for human satisfaction and soul-progress is halted.

It is, therefore, your task to cast out everything which violates love ... every critical thought (however 'justified'), every planned angry or damaging remark, everything which may cause lasting hurt. I wait for you to be victorious *every* time, in My strength.

Let My love purify your own loving instincts to make them all-embracing and constant. Make sure that, in your life, evil's divisive work among mankind is unsuccessful.

. . . the love in many will grow cold.

(Matthew 24.12)

Guard your spirit by My unfailing presence. My child, I beseech you to walk, in light, on that higher plane, where evil is powerless to influence you. I will give to you a *new direction,* focussed upon My light, as your choices are courageous for Me.

Remember that it is a special relationship between us. Not for one moment must you look, anxiously, at problems and possible demands. All these things are *dealt with* as you keep your gaze upon Me. I will not only bring about My will, but permit you, increasingly, to discern its pattern.

I want you to have the happiness of a life, though subject to many pressures and earthly discouragements, which reflects My love, My faithfulness, in your peace, your trust and your courage. Are you, very deliberately, letting Me take you

> into each day?
> into each *occasion* in that day?

I have 'taken you' into so many encounters!

I am the Good Shepherd.

(John 10.14)

My child, even at the human level there is always concern to restore a broken relationship, where you do not wish a loved one to suffer the hurt of guilt and estrangement.

Can you see, therefore, why My forgiveness is instantaneous? Even the sense of shame you bear is felt by Myself, because of My very close identification with you!

I long for all the *consequences* of estrangement to be swept away, at the very moment that you turn penitently to Me. When there is doubt, inspired by evil, about My full and free forgiveness, remember the pain to *Myself* while guilt and remorse remain in you. Remember that evil both tempts and then condemns.

I long for My love to be *felt* again, for your progress to be resumed, free of guilt's burden… for you to be happily secure in My love, with a growing obedience. What you are learning about My love will teach you much about My ways with mankind.

I have blotted out your sins;
I will not remember them.

(Isaiah 43.25)

My child, remember that My being surrounds yours. In the flesh there are inevitable dangers, and because this world is only a passing manifestation of My creation, that flesh will share in the world's weakness and eventual 'extinction'.

If you could see the potential hurts which I avert, you would indeed be lost in gratitude! Many things simply do not serve My purposes and I save you from them – even though you may not recognise them as harmful; each day you are saved from a *multitude* of such things.

My deep involvement with you is concerned with the smallest details – permitting only what is right for your eventual sanctification – and enjoyment of My near presence. I continue to work for you during both your activity and your *inactivity!*

You are of more value than many sparrows.

(Luke 12 .7)

My child, how frightening would be the future without Me when realising (as you now do), the subtle dangers of existence. *With* Me, let the thought of what lies ahead *thrill you;* do not shrink from it in any way. Upon the inevitable difficult places you will build courage, and a deeper knowledge of Myself. Each day, see the light of My presence, and the light standing over your future, as one and the same.

Your hand in Mine! . . . This is no figure of speech, but literal and very practical navigation through the uncharted areas.

Do you see My love as the only thing which matters?

> My love streaming from the realms of the Spirit . . .
> My love infiltrating the dark places of earth . . .
> Love *on* earth . . . Lifting the commonplace into heaven!

I will not leave you
without My comforting presence.

(John 14.18)

It is in order that change can occur in My children that My nature is unchanging.

A power, and an understanding upon which you can rely, provide the permanence upon which you can adventure.

New areas of conquest, new aims, new ways of thinking, represent the change in you which is based upon that which is unchanging.

Feel the divine *permanence* breaking up that which, by your own efforts, could not be broken. My purpose, revealed to mankind, of making all things new, is accomplished, as you completely rely on My changelessness.

Each day, in life's bewildering circumstances, the same love, the same power, are available to you. Because I am your hope, you know that in you lives My spirit… you will surely see its out-pouring.

Thank Me every day that you possess that which is eternal.

Before Abraham was, I AM.

(John 8.58)

Man does not see the process of renewal in those who live within My love. Yes, the spirit can die – even though, outwardly, there may appear to be strength and achievement. In time, of course, the exterior, too, must fail, and then death is complete.

To guard against death of the spirit there must be that daily inter-action of our beings . . . as prolonged, and as unaffected by the world's standards, as you can make it. My renewal of the essential person, the person whose spirit is dear to Me, carries with it the renewal, also, of many natural and visible processes. Life is then transformed into a beautiful and purposeful thing, realising the potential for which it was created.

When, eventually, the bodily processes cease, there remains a purified spirit – alive in the fullest sense, and already irrevocably linked with Me. That renewed spirit is then ready for the closer union which is My promise.

**What profit is there in gaining
the whole world and losing your soul?**
(Mark 8.36)

My child, broaden your vision of the area in which I have an influence, and in which I am able to be sufficient for every need. My love for you ensures that both in the realm of mind and spirit, and in the world of relationships and material needs, you can affirm very frequently that I am able to bring about *precisely* what I see is best for you.

There is no area from which My influence is excluded, as you keep on the narrow way.

My *interior* influence gives you the sense of peace, and the ability to contemplate the future without misgivings.

My influence *around you* – in a multiplicity of situations, and upon your time spent with people, will cause you to thank Me, with a sense of wonder, for what I have brought about.

Even if you do not see My working immediately, know that you soon *will* see where I have worked for you, and be lost in gratitude.

> **All power is given to Me . . .**
> **in heaven and on earth.**
>
> (Matthew 28.18)

I have to teach My followers submission to My will when it is *not* easy. I have to see their willingness to follow a hard road, and to make sacrifices for My sake.

When I see the submissive heart, I can show the more joyous side of My will – the restful communion with Me, the enjoyment of Myself, My gifts and My world – which I want them to have, because I love them so very much! My influence then cannot help working, and My plans going forward.

To reveal, at the outset, the many rewards of life with Me would produce the wrong motive for acceptance of My will. Only when I see unquestioning obedience, can I then shower My love and peace – and reveal the enjoyment of them as being just as truly My will as are sacrifice and duty.

If only My people had a heart which would reverence and obey Me.

(Deuteronomy 5.29)

Realise the *independence* of My activity for, and through you. I have always worked through those who have offered themselves to Me – completely independent of their recurring sense of inadequacy, their fears.

Never deny Me by feeling that an encounter was unproductive, because of your own variable sense of well-being or sureness. Do not under-value your every small act of encouragement. So often I have to show My children (by assurance given later), how *much* was achieved when they were conscious of so *little.*

My child, all this reflects in a small way My own activity when subject to earth's limitations . . . My heart full of foreboding at what lay ahead, but love able to pour through – for the revitalising of so many lives.

As a duty, thank Me at each day's end for My purposes going ahead through you – never more than when conscious of having nothing at all – except your possession of Me!

I will enable you to catch men.

(Mark 1.17)

My child, observe in the beauty of a rose, the unselfconscious *giving* of nature.

The fragrance of that flower, its delicacy, its form, its colour, have much to say to you. That flower brings delight simply by *what it is*. In the same way, your influence depends on what you *are*. Cultivating yourself to reflect My nature is the real need . . . almost the only need!

Your patience, trust, self-forgetfulness, will draw others to you; I will be *seen* at work . . . Your growth into someone whose influence for Me is great can be taken for granted as you open up yourself to My spirit's miracle-work in your heart.

The miracles in your own life are *naturally* followed by miracles wherever your influence may be felt.

Arise, let your light shine.
(Isaiah 60.1)

So many of My children, acknowledging My love, even greatly comforted by it, do not see, sufficiently, its practical aspects.

It is not merely that the thought of My love, at moments of being uplifted, helps you to be unafraid. There are more practical grounds for not being afraid of anything in your life, as you realise that My love is *actively planning* for you.

Reflect each day on this activity. Bring every discouraging factor, every apprehension, to My *active* love. To thank Me, frequently, that for you there is absolutely nothing to fear is more than brave words . . . it is the acknowledgement of a fact of our relationship.

If you could see My continuing provision and My lifting you through the periods of darkness which life may yet bring to you, you would know that to dismiss all fear truly is your *duty*. I lead you into ways of power, ways of peace.

I made you, and am able to carry you.

(Isaiah 46.4)

You cannot imagine how much I am comforted when you blindly follow My word. Your sense of My wisdom, My utter dependability, must be reflected in a corresponding following-out of My words to you.

Resist agonising conflict about My clear word and simply obey as a child. Nothing in My word will ever conflict with true wisdom. Keep the sense of *being led* by One who knows the way. Be eager to hear My Spirit's word in your heart, and then to welcome *only* what is in harmony with it.

A blind following still leaves your own perception unimpaired! You will observe this present existence with *increased* sharpness, as you resolutely keep in step with Me. After your own initial effort of choice, following My word, you will *always* find that a new area is conquered. You hold on to those gains by your complete trust in all that I am.

As it is in heaven, may Your will be carried out here on the earth.

(Matthew 6.10)

My child, because of earth's suffering, many of those who acknowledge My creative activity nevertheless feel, acutely, My remoteness. In time, this would always lead to complete unbelief.

Deeply consider again My identification, in history, with the human race. Never again could the love within the Godhead be seen as a passive love, with still a great gulf between itself and struggling humanity.

In choosing to follow Me, you show that My coming to earth was no random event, but an intervention of deepest and universal significance. Love, tenderly and patiently watching over the human race during its development, was compelled to submit to earth's experience. That experience became not only a victory in the spiritual realm, but one which is within reach of any of My children.

Since the time of My closest identification with humanity, *nothing* can prevent the fulfilment of the very natural human wish for immortality.

I came to search for the lost, and to save them.

(Luke 19.10)

Many would see an element of foolishness in My grace, a failure to ensure that My children come to grips with wrong ways, an over-indulgence of patience on My part.

How often have I made it clear that My ways are not of those of the world. Such grace as the world can produce is limited . . . and its effects limited. My grace, though seeming to make light of persistent failures, is very sure in its ultimate results.

It is the sense of My patient love – love towards the undeserving which eventually evokes in the recipients true gratitude, from which flows *more obedient lives!* What rigid law-keeping cannot produce, My love always produces . . . even though this patient process may seen unending in some lives.

My child, your growing obedience – though with many failures – points to the grace which so fully emanates from the world's Saviour . . . your life-long source of hope.

. . . until seventy-times seven!

(Matthew 18.21)

You have found the impermanence of the world's supports. You have experienced, sadly, the goodwill, but powerlessness to help, of many. I will continue to send help through human agencies, but I want you always to see Me as your very *first* resort. You can then learn to lose reliance upon earth's temporary supports.

So often, the seeking, first, of Myself as your stability in uncertainty will avoid the need of any other agency. You are then standing upon rock, and can be aware of absorbing strength from it. A rock-like quality then begins to emerge in *your own* character.

Yes, even an earthly rock can disintegrate but you have fixed your hope upon the rock of history… being, for you, what it has been for so many…

Unshakeable, and *instantly* accessible!

I will strengthen you.

(Judges 6.14)

Where there are problems which seem insoluble, My children so often make the mistake of 'trying' too hard – even after a matter has been committed to Me. There is the temptation to force solutions by over-activity, or over-persuasion.

Wisdom is merely to do what *reasonably* can be done – within a life which is covered by prayer. Only when the wisdom which I have given you shows it to be necessary must you act decisively.

Matters which seem so complex or obstinate are, of course, very different in My sight; . . . they would only remain as 'problems' if they were not given to Me!

Therefore, you can have absolute confidence in My handling of every difficult situation, My completion of 'unfinished business' in wonderful ways . . . as you, for your part, gladly walk in My way.

According to your faith may it happen for you!

(Matthew 9.29)

Avoid both undue elation and undue depression of spirit – which are tied to outward conditions; you do this by finding your satisfaction in My companionship, My loyalty to you, rather than in the things of the senses, or in temporary good fortune.

Always have in mind *joyfully* when contemplating the future, that the way ahead is *with Me*. Observe all that I have told you . . . these truths do not change. Do not give time to vain imaginings! Just be concerned with My cause on this earth . . . let all your energy pour into this. Simply step out in that new quality of life which truly is yours.

My child, are you *really* confident about My good influence upon your life? You know the way which leads to My Kingdom; as you have found, you are not without severe pressure to step aside from that way! Do not let external circumstances, or any demands upon you – entice you into allowing the things which spell danger.

. . . troubled about so many things!

(Luke 10.41)

My child, are you remembering to let My love be the environment in which you walk without fear? Fear can cripple your life, preventing the full work of sanctification, compelling you to act with disastrous consequences, both for yourself and for others.

Do not tolerate another day in which fear rules, or even partially rules. I long to see you leave fear behind permanently . . . as a response to My love. Trust Me, with absolute abandon, in defying evil's pressure to act fearfully. Do not let misgivings, or dread of consequences, cause you to retreat, after your fearless choice.

Let the dominant sense of My love, and your actions against fear go together. If fear is followed, it will always dim My light. Courageous choices (if you are careful that there is no hurt to Me) will be seen to have been wise choices!

Be courageous and strong.

(Joshua 1.6)

When there is a time of change in your life, moves about to be made affecting your future, go forward very quietly, and test everything by the light of My presence. I will let nothing take you astray; facing changes, base *everything* upon your certainty of My love.

Meet all choices with that glance to Me; . . . let Me weave them into My will. Contemplating any action, remember the look to My love, and the *pause* – to see My heavenly corroboration! Let your growing wisdom influence events.

Confronting complexities, keeping close to Me is all that matters. Circumstances then harmonise... both in yours and in others' lives which concern you. My wishes in those puzzling choices will just naturally be carried out . . . You know that you can rely on Me to open or close doors!

Follow Me!

(Matthew 4.19)

Where else could you find a completely new start so *quickly* after bringing yourself into a frightening or 'hopeless' situation?

Where else could you find even your foolish and wrong ways, repented over, actually made into a *positive* starting point for fresh endeavour?

The sense that you can pick yourself up and start again, the ability to emerge from a sombre into a hopeful frame of mind, just by being with Me, is something which the world cannot give to you.

Through history, when trusted, I have righted wrongs, quieted anxious spirits, turned sorrow into joy, imparted strength to begin again, after devastating failures.

My child, you realise that you must always come to Me for *renewal* . . . in its widest possible sense.

**Your sins may be like scarlet,
but they shall be as white as snow.**

(Isaiah 1.18)

ou know that I am at work all the time…
purposefully and unhurriedly. To follow My
pattern, you, too, must make use of each
moment. Reflecting more of My love and My
wisdom, you will advance My purposes. Not all
will be 'activity'; much will be a loving and patient
influence; much will be a giving to Me, as you
rest in Me.

The use of each moment means ensuring that I
am *in*volved . . .

    . . . reaching others through you
    . . . inspiring you
    . . . receiving from you.

You may feel that your contribution is
insignificant, compared with the whole. You must
know that your involvement of Myself is a
furthering of My purposes which is out of all
proportion to the willingness, and trustfulness,
of the single life concerned.

My child, just abandon your life to My continuous
involvement . . . and its marvellous use in My
creative plans.

I am the Vine; you are the branches.

(John 15.5)

*T*he world looks at My followers to see if I am reflected, to see if being My follower makes a *difference* . . . to see if there is that unmistakable quality of hope, to see if there is patient love shown in every circumstance.

More than argument, reflecting Me overcomes natural resistance, and draws the spirit of another child of Mine towards Me. Your influence for Me must not be frantic, nor compulsive.

Involved in serving Me is much unspectacular and tedious work, carried out faithfully, but *always* My work is being carried out where I am seen, unselfconsciously, in a life, ensuring the *attraction* of My love in the world around. I work through you *where you are.*

Have you put yourself completely at My disposal? As you share life with Me, everything which you do for Me is *unaffected* by the barriers which the world appears to erect!

Let your light shine for people around!

(Matthew 5.16)

My child, observe the *unifying* aspect of My love . . . it is in that love that you serve... and it is in the same love that you rest!

In My love, I reached out to draw you along the road leading to oneness with Me . . . a oneness which must be *your* ambition!

Thinking much of My love, you can be:
    unburdened ...
    confident ...
    tranquil ...
    full of hope ...
    secure from evil ...
    filled with love for others ...
    wise ...
    patient...
    all-conquering ...

When the demands of life are very great, keep within the circle of our love relationship . . . let that relationship *always* disperse guilt, fear, agitation of spirit.

My love for you will be limitless.

(Hosea 14.4)

Instead of alarm when temptation is fierce, *welcome* the temptation as an opportunity for proving My liberating power! Evil will contest your growing obedience and union with Myself; I cannot remove all temptation from you, but will *only* permit what will assist your spiritual growth.

To exercise your freedom in sudden temptations, maintain the life of calm, and of a joyful spirit. Your failures to resist temptation have, of course, held up your progress and brought sorrow to My heart . . . Remember that look away to Me, establishing your *new status* in that moment of need.

How petty is evil's opposition! Watch its influence decline as you surrender to Mine.

If you contemplate your own intermittent gains (and falls!) you can so easily become disheartened. This need never be so – if you remember that your entire hope is always in what *I* am. As we march together, evil cannot keep you from attaining.

Be alert, and pray.

(Matthew 26.41)

My child, there are many roads to My friendship, but the *royal* road is that of being rescued from complete darkness . . . brought into a realm of light and hope – and with a sense of being cared for.

No experience is quite like the recognition of one's helplessness – and then to find a way through, with Me. Never lose an opportunity of telling what I have done for you and what I mean to you. I will send those opportunities! Speak of the Friend who cannot be defeated; speak of the *hugeness* of My mercy and My patience.

I am already, in love, reaching out to rescue the child who turns helplessly, and only half-believing, to Me; as that child does so, I can *already experience* the thankfulness of that child at having found the Lord of all history.

Return to Me . . .
I have bought your freedom!

(Isaiah 44.22)

Men have been slow to see that a relationship with Me is built upon their coming to the One who is *already there*.

Be very thankful that you saw the need merely to allow yourself to be lifted into My *existing* presence – rather than vainly seeing Me as apart from you, needing to be persuaded to break into your life. Through My Spirit you began to desire Me . . . all that I could be to you, and could give to you, were built into your life.

My promises about never leaving you – many in number – must always reassure you, even when bitterly ashamed or thoroughly discouraged about your spiritual journey. My love makes it imperative for Me to remain deeply involved with your existence.

No external 'observances' can ever help you to draw closer . . . only, perhaps, to *appreciate* that closeness. It is My immanent presence which *prompts* you to turn instinctively to Me in absolutely any circumstances.

Soon I will leave the world, but will come again to you.

(John 14.18-19)

You see how My love not only forms a protective ring around you, but also affects, by its presence, all mental activity, and the ways in which your existence touches what is in the world. It is love which gives life, love which revolutionises life.

I want you to notice My love's influence . . . upon thinking; in the victories you win; in bringing about your responses where everything else has failed.

My child, how I long for you to know even more of that love! Within My love you will come safely through many dark places... even though in times of weakness, this may seem impossible for you. Meeting those dark places with Me, *your* life becomes a place where My purposes for this world move towards fulfilment.

How could I, your Friend, let you down?

Whoever overcomes will inherit all things.

(Revelation 21.7)

Be God-centred at all times . . . ideally prepared to see the way which you must follow.

Avoid preoccupation with self, which gives an opening to evil . . . self-concern can so easily become habitual . . . one of the more subtle forms of sin, causing the person indulging in it no anxiety! . . . *Turn from* apprehension and preoccupation with self and *turn to* someone else's need, or to an interest outside self.

The task is always to see that *your* life is right – whatever may seem to be the defects of those around you. It is only as you obey, that more light from Me can be shed upon your path.

To know My power – even to commend it to others – is never enough; there must be utterly-trusting choices in reversing the old life of self. Do not waste our friendship; just keep your anchor fixed in Me.

Look to Me . . . and be saved.

(Isaiah 45.22)

My child, the refusal of anxiety, now that you are so firmly in My hands.... You give anxiety the soil in which to grow whenever you look away from Me, and survey your situation from a very human and limited viewpoint.

Prolonged and futile anxiety creates the climate for many *other* temptations, of which you are only too aware. When evil tries to implant anxious thoughts, stand upon Me and refuse them. Turn anxieties into opportunities!

Engross yourself with others' needs from the right motive (the motive of love), ensuring that less of your mind's energy is being poured into self and its needs – real or imagined.

Can you literally *feel* yourself thinking and acting in new ways . . . refusing all that is not of calm and patience? Because you have been rescued from the power of darkness, you can simply let Me rob *all* anxieties of their power.

Consider the lilies of the field!

(Matthew 6.28)

Dwell much upon those of whom I have spoken as truly blessed. Covet the qualities which they show; then, let Me bring *you* into the company of those who have allowed their lives to be transformed by My loving control.

Remember My promise that My suffering ones will know *My* compensation; that those showing compassion and forgiveness earn My own tender love and My deep understanding.

My strength will ensure your following the example set by My blessed ones You need not look, constantly, to see whether their virtues have become yours . . . just know that as you covet those qualities and absorb yourself greatly with Me, *all* are being developed in you.

With Me as both Goal and Companion on your journey, you are sure of reaching My promised realm, even though this earth's conditions may appear to your finite mind as obstacles!

**In My Father's Kingdom,
good people will shine like the sun.**

(Matthew 13.43)

A sense of 'lightness' . . . burdens *really* given over to Me! What you are able to do for Me must never be affected by what you are carrying needlessly, – failing to trust My power and My wisdom. How much suffering is caused by lack of trust – a suffering which I am forced to share, as I long for the partial to become perfect in you.

See the relationship between trusting and peace. I am able to bring about that which is above all you could possibly envisage. Reflect more upon My greatness! . . . when burdened, turn to My *greatness,* and receive the strength and renewal you need – without question.

Do not take back any of the matters which you have committed to Me . . . I, your Lord, am aware of every recurring doubt, but deep within you, there is bound to be the growing certainty of *attainment* . . . My plans for you *are* being perfected.

Do not be concerned about tomorrow.

(Matthew 6.34)

Remember that there are two aspects of My word.

Firstly, there is the call to obedience – pointing the way which will keep you from straying into danger, the way which will mean your eventual true joy; then, there is the *atmosphere created* by My word. If you have come, often, to My word you will know that it not only challenges, but *gives*.

My word is always a *contemporary* word and infiltrates those complex circumstances, or struggles, of the moment.

My child, to expose yourself to My word *must* bring hope, even in the darkest places. The strength which is taken into you when living in My word means that My commands can be seen, once more, as being within your grasp.

Do not deprive yourself of absorbing the atmosphere of My Kingdom; allow My word to heal your spirit. Healing is *always* accomplished for you as you stand upon Me, trusting My word, and believing in all that I have done for you.

The words I speak are Spirit-filled and mean life.

(John 6.63)

My child, you are sure that I oversee the whole span of your life; whatever unfolds now is being shaped, because of your trust, into a meaningful pattern for the days ahead. I stand there at the unknown future, exerting My influence, which is invincible.

Because the love cannot be broken, you must be certain that My provision, My protection, are yours – as of right – in the coming days.

Remember that the material is only a minor part of existence. When there is much which you cannot understand of My *present* working, just reflect upon My knowledge of, and influence in, your future. Let this give you an unparalleled sense of security, and an absence of all that is motivated by fear.

The revealing of the world's Creator in a manner leaving no possible doubt is something which you can eagerly anticipate!

Your sun will never set!

(Isaiah 60.20)

My child, existence has many deceptions, assailing your spirit through a variety of channels. Never be afraid to confront truth and, with Me, to live by it, whatever the cost. My truths all harmonise, one with another.

Without Me you are at the mercy of lies fed to the mind by evil, causing so much human unhappiness. Under evil's influence, the world will flatter you, make you angry, confuse you, or make you deviate from My path ... all with disastrous results.

When the *central* truth of My love, is accepted, warmly, you acquire the skill of recognising what is false or dangerous. The world's deceptions now cause you sorrow, and you become determined not to be led by them; what is false or dangerous is *also* recognised when it invades your own mental processes!

Subject everything to the test of My truth. I give to you the capacity to do this. Whatever does not harmonise with the fundamental truth of My existence and of My love, must not be allowed to exist in you.

The way is narrow which leads to life.

(Matthew 7.14)

My child, remember the practical activity of *sharing* which is involved in our all-important friendship. The hurts which you feel, I feel to an infinitely greater degree. Your moments of being uplifted, moments when hope returns, rejoice My heart more than you could imagine.

See Me going before you, prospering every good intention, preparing hearts for your meeting with them, ensuring that in everything you will not be harmed. A friendship which did not share in this way would not be worthy of the name. I experience the light and shade of your life at every moment, every temptation conquered, every warm instinctive act towards another, every choosing of Myself (rather than the world) for help.

It means much to Me that you share My life, and can reach into, and bring joy to, My own heart.

I have called you . . . friends.
(John 15.15)

My love *must* now cause you to walk in ways which are undeflected by evil . . . a walk which is not intermittent! At moments of choice, moments of conflict, I am *hurt* by your doubt and fear, when there should be belief in My victory, and My complete protection.

I leave in your hands the *appropriation* of My victory; I will seal it for you. Expect evil to oppose My work, in you, of sanctification. I permit this opposition *for the moment.* Evil plans your destruction, but will be unable to produce its devastating consequences as you trust, and as you keep in the light of My presence.

As you look away from self, and towards Me or towards My other children, you can *know* that your new walk has begun. I uphold you as you go from one victory to the next. Yes, my child, it is a struggle . . . but one in which I am shaping you into a victorious person, bringing great glory to My name.

New wine is not put into old bottles.

(Matthew 9.17)

Because of our *closeness, you* can steel yourself to tread the road which I have shown you . . . Involved in our closeness is that sense of purpose, that sense of future . . . you tread a road with many dangers, but leading to the privileged enjoyment of an eternity spent in helping to bring about My purposes.

The atmosphere of heaven is around you, because of our unity. Your effort in any direction is unfailingly assisted. Even when you are not conscious of any intention, My activity is present. Our closeness *used* means that evil cannot intrude.

Remain aware of the basis of love upon which our unity rests, the love-sense ensuring that there is a constant movement towards your spiritual vocation being fulfilled. My child, our closeness is a *fact* . . . reflect upon it frequently!

Do not be afraid; I accompany you.

(Isaiah 41.10)

True worship is not a matter of words . . . except those which spring from a *thankful* heart. True worship is a sense of awe concerning Myself, deeply felt, and which cannot be fully contained in what is external or man-devised.

The *continuity* of worship throughout each day, with a sense of My presence which never leaves you . . . this is no impossible ideal! Worship's continuity . . . your heart lifted above earthly things, is broken by every thought, word or action not in harmony with that adoration which you express in your highest moments.

My love must always draw out your worship. The sheer gratitude of worship follows naturally from the growing experience of all that I can be to you in a dark world.

Spend each day, irrespective of its details, in a worship which is childlike, extravagent, and free from fear.

Able to worship only by His Spirit.

(John 4.24)

My child, knowledge of Me is thought to be impossible, even by many who claim to believe. I am seen as either the grudging rewarder of those who stoically endure this life, or as One who very partially reveals Himself to the ethically-advanced. It is My love's ordaining that experience of *life itself* brings a growing knowledge of Me whenever I have been sought; knowledge found in:

> Each glimpse of hope in suffering;
> Each tender understanding with another;
> Each intimation of companionship in solitude;
> Each experience of safety in dangerous places;
> Each upsurge of previously-absent courage.

The only danger is that I am not *acknowledged* in these things. If you believe that My presence is immanent, and My ways discoverable, then you will gain a deep knowledge of the world's Saviour from countless facets of this present life.

I am the Light of the World.

(John 8.12)

The sense of being renewed each day is so much part of living with Me. How often you have been aware of being saved from the consequences of your own foolishness and selfishness, of being lifted clear of those consequences to a place where you can almost hear Me saying "Yes, you can start again!"

My forgiveness *makes new*; My peace *makes new*.

'Renewal' from earthly sources is limited, conditional upon so many things; *My* renewal is your birthright as a trusting child, growing in knowledge of My way.

I bring a new factor in relationships, a new factor in long-standing problems, when I am allowed to enter. Nothing is more precious for you than the new beginnings which you enjoy . . . new beginnings which steadily reduce those times of failure... new beginnings which shorten, drastically, the effects of the failures which *do* occur!

Bring the finest robe and put it on him!
(Luke 15.22)

To discover your helplessness without Me is a process which I allow, repeatedly, until the lesson is learned.

A brittle self-confidence can, of course, be acquired, but your basic inadequacy must be crystal-clear, if you have been willing to see My truth. It is your confidence in *Me* which enables you to act victoriously, even when feeling anything but strong.

There is a direct relation between remorse in failure and weakness, and finding yourself with a firmer hold upon My love. Nowhere is My love so overwhelmingly experienced than at moments of self-realisation… seeing yourself as you are – and then the privileged sight of Myself as I am.

At times when you remembered to use My strength (and at times when you failed to use it!) there remained the *constant* factor of My love. It is *this* love which ensures that your feeling of utter dependency can be seen by the world around you as strength! This will draw others to Me, unfailingly.

Come back . . . and I will heal you.

(Jeremiah 3.22)

It may seem incredible to those who only partially see the meaning of my universe, but *each one* of My children is precious to Me. My sadness is that, for so many reasons, there is no knowledge of Me.

You readily see how precious is a child to the most devoted parent – even when that child rejects or hurts the love shown. Compared with even *this* love, My own is beyond your comprehension.

My child, reflect on how precious *you* are to Me. Take satisfaction that My sadness in rejection, (because of your trust) is not present between us.

My joy in My creation is so much *enhanced* by every child who, in the simplest dependence, comes to unite his or her life with Mine.

You did not choose Me . . . I chose you!

(John 15 .16)

As part of My revelation to the world, I have spoken to many hearts . . . chosen by Me to make known My purposes. The spirit-breathed word has been expressed through many channels, and no generation has been left without clear knowledge of Myself and of My ways.

The main purpose of My word, before My appearing on earth, was to prepare for that perfect revelation of the Godhead through Myself. That word has now a new dimension... that of fulfilment (My love has been *seen;* God's victory has been *experienced)* I still speak, by My Spirit, to those who wish to know Me, and to be used by Me.

Until the awareness of the spiritual reality behind existence fully comes, I bequeath all that is needed for a trusting child . . . I give knowledge and hope . . . I give that priceless sense of never being alone in a creation which moves painfully, but surely, towards its highest purposes.

I am the bright and morning Star.

(Revelation 22.16)

You will be glad, increasingly, that you "decided upon Me", or, rather, that I drew you to Myself! You realise that an ordered life *is* possible. Already you have seen how trust has been repaid; in other matters you still have to wait!

I know the continuing pressures upon your life, the areas of weakness which those pressures still find out. Nevertheless these weaknesses need not overcome you because you have *proved* that there is victory in all these things. A growing obedience will mean that restlessness and agitation will simply melt away . . . still keep very close, and follow the impulse which I give you as you look submissively – and affectionately – in My direction.

Having absorbed My word, let your *life* now tell the world that I cannot fail you in anything. You will see My will unfold, wonderfully, in your life.

To observe all that I have commanded you.

(Matthew 28.20)

Does your life show the *advancement* of My influence . . much *more* of Me – and much less of the old, failing self?

My child, do not despise many of the things in your nature which are of Me; in expressing them, you are fulfilling the plan of life which has been made, uniquely, for you. At the same time, let it be an *urgent* discipline to ensure that there is much room for Me . . . replacing the self-referred and unloving ways which I have given you the capacity to recognise. Never let evil make you lower your standards.

Newness of life is *fact,* not rhetoric; it involves the expansion of My life in you, and the extinction of all that delays My purposes. My child, I am making *new* lives of trusting ones all the time.

We will make our home in him.

(John 14.23)

Peace such as the world cannot give . . . My child, you realise that this is no empty phrase. The *creativeness* of My peace must be understood.

> Peace preparing the way for wise action, finding ways to overcome those 'insoluble' problems; reaching others, and drastically changing their circumstances.

Peace is the gift which I have always desired for My children. The first intimations of that peace are when I am found; . . . it then grows within the heart of one who ascends, with Me, the steps of the life of the Spirit. My child, look into My countenance of love . . . hating (with Me) all that can destroy peace   including those things in you which still need to be cast out. Let My peace flood your whole being.

In My presence, now . . . peace!

**I am the Shepherd of My sheep,
and cause them to rest.**

(Ezekiel 34.15)

How I grieve to see so many of My children led, in various paths, away from safety... away from Me.

Because there is real freedom of will, I cannot always enforce a return to safety, but I do *pursue*... I never tire of making it possible for a choice to be made to return home.

I pursue in *far* wanderings from My way. I also pursue when one of My children, (as yourself), wanders even *slightly* into danger. This is why you feel the uneasiness, the loss of peace, which accompanies the straying from My way.

My child, rejoice that there is in you, instinctively, the desire to return quickly to *Me* when losing the sense of My presence, and a sense of the purposeful direction in which you were travelling.

Are you now *convinced* that only the way I have shown to you will satisfy your deepest longings?

I have found My sheep which was lost.

(Luke 15.6)

Without me, one is a prisoner in this world. Even those who see themselves as free and independent in spirit, are greatly limited; they are shaped by their environment and their circumstances far more than they realise.

Real freedom carries you over the world's many restrictions – once I have been used as the door to new life. All other promised entrances to freedom and happiness are false. I alone am the entrance to the security and *peace* of the heavenly kingdom. The door of life is kept open for all who wish to enter; it then becomes a door of safety – *closed* against the permanent harm which the world could inflict upon a child living in My presence.

Let many share with you the knowledge of where real life is entered into . . . I am the *only* way.

I am the Door.
(John 10.9)

My children can go so far astray from Me if they fail to live by what I have revealed to them. There are countless instances in this world of tampering with truth in order to secure advantage. You can fall into this same trap. If you live by the fact of My unchanging love, holding fast to it at all costs, no power on earth can deflect you.

Never compromise with the truth established in your heart, when under pressure by evil. Never let your convictions and your highest ideals be at variance with the way in which you live out your present existence; this weakens the store of truth which governs your actions. Compromise is so easy, but the road back to My path after compromise, involves the putting right of so much misfortune and the removal of so many barriers to progress. If the voice of truth within is put aside – even temporarily – the price is too great.

All who love the truth are My followers.

(John 18.37)

One of life's most painful states is that of feeling completely misunderstood.

Ask Me for the *permanent* awareness that I understand perfectly, all that motivates you, and all that, from time to time, brings hurt to Myself... an understanding which extends to what you have brought upon yourself by self-will, and by forgetfulness of Me.

My child, My understanding is based on love, rather than on the cynicism with which the world makes its judgements. Even from the closest human source you need not seek that which is there for you precisely when needed. You can always be sure of *one* source of understanding and that will be enough. This will set you free to enter into communion with Me with complete frankness.

After failure, never doubt the pardoning aspect of that understanding – to know that you are *really* understood means genuine spiritual progress.

I will heal all that they have done and love them freely.

(Hosea 14.4)

Status of the worldly kind does not bring lasting satisfaction . . . only the sense of My love can do this.

Your status depends on something infinitely more precious – our friendship. Knowledge that you are valued by many, or greatly used, is beyond price.

My child, anything which feeds the self can come between us; the world's transient glory cannot be compared with our lasting friendship. Consciousness of status in My service is far more deadly than in a worldly context. Do not strive after status . . . or even covet it.

My approval of that longing for Me in your heart is all that you need to feed upon!

The last shall be first; the first last.

(Luke 13.30)

A few steps into compromise, and often it is as if all hell is let loose upon you, as events become out of control, that precious walk with Me temporarily lost.

Because the way is narrow it does not mean that you have to walk in fear. There is a wealth of things which I permit upon that way. Learn now, the immediate return to the narrow way, should you have strayed. It is for your good that you are made to realise, from time to time, that you cannot control even the most insignificant events which your life can embrace.

You realise that I am in control of *all* things and you must enjoy allowing Me to be so! Surrendering, consciously, to *My* control is the great opening for My peace to be experienced. Has the wonderful truth about that new way *really* dawned upon you?

You must be perfect!

(Matthew 5.48)

When you give way to complaining about your situation, it may seem a small thing, but it is giving an entrance to evil . . . far more hurtful in its consequences than would have seemed possible when you indulged in the luxury of 'the little grumble', 'the little complaint'.

I have ordained it so. Life with Me demands a trust and joy which must not be broken, because the results of breaking them are so bad. Never be lured into pessimistic or gloomy utterance, whatever the provocation; this further lowers your spirits and leaves you open to so many other temptations, holding up the answers to your prayers. The forces of evil are infinitely cunning in exploiting your situation.

You realise that the need to walk in new ways is one of urgency. Only the trusting and joyful way which I have urged will keep out the pressure of evil.

I will give you a new heart and a new spirit.
(Ezekiel 36.26)

My child, you realise that those wishing to be channels of My love must be *unobstructed* channels.

It is not a condition of My using you that you feel strong, full of faith and in control at all times! It is, however, an *automatic* condition that you are not clinging to anything which hurts My patient love for you. In such a case, that which is harmful rather than helpful may come from contacts which you have. The pollution of something alien to Myself can be in those contacts.

Avoid what would affect your service by letting My love feed you, and by *rapid* recognition of false bypaths. The remedy is always submission… surrendering what you know in your heart to be wrong. No child of Mine is without some obstruction to the free flow of My love and My power. Your vital task is ensuring that when it is most needed (in another's need), that flow can be full and spontaneous.

If your right eye makes you go astray, pluck it out.

(Matthew 5.29)

My child, remember, always, the dependability of a promise made out of Divine love . . . and founded upon My omnipotence. When tempted to doubt whether I can be depended upon for victory in a difficult area, think much of My love, the promise-source.

My love means the strongest possible desire for you to emerge from being a defeated person into one who achieves much . . . both in the realm of personality, and in realms beyond yourself. Patiently allow Me to bring your affairs into harmony. You may not always detect My work of promise – fulfilment, nor the moments of My perfect intervention. Just see the unchanging nature of that love as indicating the absolute sureness of all that I promise about power for living. An attitude of resting in My love *is* newness of life!

There is no other Saviour.

(Isaiah 43.11)

It is vital to learn the attitude of –
banking upon Me.

Bank on Me for love and forgiveness – always;

Bank on Me for the imparting to you of wisdom;

Bank on Me as your partner – blessing and
completing everything upon which you embark
according to My purpose;

Bank on Me for loving communion;

Bank on Me as your understanding Friend, who
can never give you other than encouragement.

Do you wish to ensure that the promises you
have made to Me are kept? Then bank upon My
strength, keeping within the light of My presence.
Break down the barriers between us, so that your
vision of My love becomes clear.

Great victories are won, during times of challenge
and testing, in the lives of those who *really* bank
upon Me!

When you pass through fire, it will not burn you.

(Isaiah 43.2)

My child, remember the power for living which you possess as you consciously walk in My light, and My freedom; *value* the freedom which is yours and use it consistently.

Do not be surprised at the conflicts around and within you, nor at the great pressures of evil upon you. Evil knows that, keeping close to Me, you are on a victory path, from which nothing can remove you; you cannot be overwhelmed. Do not let evil induce guilt or fear. *Convert* its assaults, its lies, into victories.

Be bold in your choices for Me and, having chosen, refuse all misgivings! Your growing courage will be based on the fact that I am not failing you. Let the world see what My power in you, My conquest of evil, can achieve. Yes, My child, you have a *real* freedom.

I will let no-one oppose you.

(Joshua 1.5)

It is My Spirit in you which whispers "All is well" when life's fluctuations seem to proclaim a loveless creation. My Spirit is your *light,* unseen by the world, but with effects unmistakable in a life which can rise above everything which is limiting. My light beckons you forward . . . do not look back with regret or self-pity.

Your hopeful look towards Me is really your *assent* to all that I am doing in your heart. Although you may not always see this work occurring, it has assured consequences. Ensure that My Spirit's working is unfettered and continuous by that unwavering *desire* for Me... and by that *absolute* trust in My promises.

Be, in the truest sense, a child of the Spirit! For such a child, everything which is at present tangled, or fear-provoking, *must* be made right.

Whatever may be happening around you, always *rejoice* that you are in My care. This is the true and only antidote to the fears of mankind.

My Spirit will never leave you.

(Isaiah 59.21)

As you keep close to Me, *know* that we are one... This means that you are allied to My purposes, that you share in My working. Remember to *see* us as united ... to know that there is *an influence from us* when with others. You can therefore, rely upon the *influence*, rather than upon striving. You must keep your eyes upon the *goal* - which is *possession of Myself*, both by yourself and by others. This will remove, automatically, striving about worldly things.

Always be ready to go where I send you. Some need will *confront you* ... never turn away from it. Simply be My hands and eyes, wherever you are, available for those whom I show to you. You have My promise that opportunities will *come* to you as the walk with Me in newness of life is cultivated. You will surely see My outworking in others' lives.

**By your love
people will know that you are My disciples.**

(John 13.35)

My child, remember that you must let My love be the answer to everything . . .

Lost in My love . . .
Looking nowhere but to My love . . .

Learn to see everything in your experience as *encompassed* by My love. Seeing all against the background of My love . . . that love transforming the effects of circumstances.

The attitude of keeping, consciously, within My protective love has to become a *discipline,* an absolute necessity. That ever-present sense of My love will give you increasing joy. Move without haste so that My promises may be brought to fruition.

My thoughts towards you are those of peace.

(Jeremiah 29. 11)

When, because of a person's attentiveness to Me, and trust in Me, I am *involved* in a life, this is always a *miracle –* involvement. Where, through the consent of a person, My influence is at work this becomes one further extension of the rule of God. Miraculous changes are then automatic both in the life of that person and others with whom he or she is in contact. The miraculous is brought about by the realisation of My closeness!

The help you receive is increasingly recognised as Mine ... the moving of hearts, the blessing of each effort. Looking to Me and seeking My wisdom it is as if I Myself am acting ... you are truly My partner in shaping events. Your prayers for others ensure My wearing down of evil's influence in their hearts.

**Whoever believes in Me
will be performing what I perform.**

(John 14.12)

It is a question of believing the very best of Me in a world which may seem, at times, as if I had abandoned it. Try to show Me as the complete answer to *any* person's need. Feed My lambs …

Because My love has never changed, My *activity* has not ceased. So many have restricted My activity in their lives by turning away from the path of faith and expectancy.

It is always wisdom to grasp My promises, and to listen to no other voice. I came to gladden the hearts of all who look only to Me. In My presence, surrendered to Me, your own thoughts can be relied upon, increasingly, as from Me.

Do you now believe?

(John 16.31)

You cannot escape the *effort* of choice – the action – which *establishes* victory. As you choose My way, victory is *always* there for you, and you will not find Me to fail.

Because of the desperate urgency to walk in newness of life, I give to you, in My love, renewed power to regain lost ground . . . evil rendered powerless. Rely on Me – absolutely – to make you aware of hurt to Me, and then to complete the victory.

My child, allow no piercing of your defences. I want you to experience, the trusting walk (entered into, in the fullest sense) for the first time.

My way forward ... using your wisdom, showing courage, and avoiding all that is of self-motivation.

Protect them from the evil one.

(John 17.15)

When a course of yours would hurt Me, there will be a vivid sense of unease as you look to Me . . . a *clouding of My love.* The sense of our being victorious together will be absent. If a course is hurtful to Me, for *any* reason, lack of peace will persist, if you are intent upon My will.

Remember the pressure of evil towards both sin and fear, and make each occasion of evil's activity one of victory with Me. Experience both My peace, and My promised strength, as you do so. Move with freedom in My light, relying upon the warning voice within, to arrest you at time of danger. I will show you, clearly what is wrong, but avoid the *overburdened* conscience and fear of consequences. You must not allow evil to paralyse you when your heart is given to Me and My will is uppermost.

Whoever follows truth will walk in My light.

(John 3 .21)

My child desire *only* truth . . .

Remember that when truth prevails *now,* it saves endless later misunderstandings. Therefore allow Me to take things in *My* direction and see Me wonderfully bring about My will. You simply
relax in My wisdom,
learn sensitivity to My working.

Do not forget that *all* hearts can be moved by Me, and that, with Me, the darkness will always be illuminated.

You can safely allow *events* to show you the way forward, as long as there is My *corresponding witness* within your own heart.

My work for you is *assisted* as you cultivate the person I wish you to be, and as everything is done in newness of life.

Love the truth.

(Zechariah 8.19)

$\mathbf{C}$an you not sense that I am at work? I cannot overlook anything which is for your good. I am active all the time in everything which you have committed to Me; this means that you must continue with utter trust in Myself. Be conscious of My constant influence:

> peace-giving ...
> affecting relationships ...
> 'making right' ....

Keep very close, as we meet life's situations as *partners*, and as you are led to that which I have planned for you. You must *feel* our unity . . .

Let Me be increasingly precious to you – My Fatherhood, My understanding, My constant activity for you.

> The way of love ...
> Love from yourself ...
> Love *between us* ...

Turn to Me with all your heart.

(Joel 2.12)

My child, I allow you to see the sheer darkness within from time to time; this is so that you may know the extent to which evil can infiltrate. But remember that your heart is towards Me. Therefore, sinful ways, repented over, are consigned to where they are powerless to affect the future.

You must always thank Me that My love has completely swallowed up the wrong and that there remains *only* My love.

When evil attempts to make you re-live occasions of sin, when it uses circumstances to try to produce renewed guilt and fear, affirm very strongly My forgiveness, as I *shield you* against evil's accusing voice.

**There is joy in heaven
over one sinner who repents.**

(Luke 15.10)

Has the lesson of resting in My love in *every* situation been learned?

As my love surrounds you – assisted by your resting attitude – everything which takes place within it is serving My purposes. Therefore, peace can prevail and thankfulness.

Remember that the way to victory is the rigid looking to Me, letting My strength be applied, and seeing the area of weakness or difficulty yield to My presence. Always apply My presence *early...*

Be content to let Me lead . . . which may mean the putting aside of plans, hastily formed, in which there was not the clear awareness of My urging. If I am at work for you the *pace* must be Mine, so that harmony prevails. Do nothing out of fear as I supply your needs in *My* way.

Learn of Me.

(Matthew 11.29)

Always be careful to walk in the known way – that which I have revealed to you. As you firmly obey My *known* wishes, you can then confidently let Me lead the way in the problem areas. I know that you will keep your hand in Mine in the uncharted places, and remember the *power of your prayers,* about both people and circumstances. When a course is open for you, having sought My will, do not be hindered by misgivings. Do not try to 'solve' every matter before taking that step with Me.

Utter straightforwardness, seeking simplicity. Nothing in your walk must be complex or in any way devious. Ensure your *direction* of travel, seeing all as either helping or hindering your forward march. If *love* is present – for Me and My children – there is no hindrance to perceiving truth.

**Whoever carries out God's will,
will know the truth of His teaching.**

(John 7.17)

Do not 'feed' self in any way. Remove the motivations of self by bringing them under My victory. *Immediately* let the energy poured into self pour, instead, into concern about Me, your pleasing of Me, our communion. Let that energy flow outwards in both concern and ingenuity about others' needs.

Looking away, looking away …

Praising …

Trusting in *My* meeting of your needs …

An iron discipline is needed, using My victory, so that you do not strive in anything motivated by self; this will ensure that the flow to others is unhindered. You will be helped by seeing Me *coming between you* and the pressure by evil to focus upon self and its needs. My child, as you surrender to Me, you can watch the old self-referred ways go out of your life, evil having to retreat.

Whoever loves his life will lose it.

(John 12.25)

Carry no burdens, except the responsibility of loving Me and serving Me. There must be no apprehension, as you simply let Me lead, and as you see My hand in events; the constant surrender to My love – ensuring your peace, and influencing events – even when you are conscious of recent sinful ways.

Now more than ever, you can allow My *leading* – experiencing the results of My working – both in surrounding events, and in My strength to respond to those events successfully. There are constant attempts by evil to destroy your peace. Do not listen to its lies. Never feel that you are at the mercy of the old ways – that is denying Me.

You have victory over evil, and therefore you must use it, treading My way of joy and courage, no matter what the circumstances.

I saw Satan fall from heaven, like lightning.

(Luke 10.18)

My love …
resolving all conflicts
meeting all needs
watching over each of your affairs.
It is love *without limit* … a very active love on
your behalf.

Continue to deliberately let all go in My love, as
I go before you. Every need the subject of prayer,
and My strengthening for life's demands,
constantly drawn upon.

Surrender in the everyday choices is *always*
established by My victory. Let your willingness
and sacrifice produce a radical change now, as
the former ways are simply relinquished.

Ask Me for an increase of love . . .
love for those associated with you,
love for all who may receive through you.

**Be faithful unto death so that you may
receive a crown of life.**

(Revelation 2.10)

Let peace reign . . .

As you continue to rest in My love, allow that love to strengthen you to obey. Yes, *enveloped* in My love ... this is always your immediate need.

Remembering to *use* My presence ....
Glorifying My Name ...
My hands *your* hands ...
My *moulding* ...
Reflecting Me ...

Let there be much silence . . . ensuring that communion with Me, and with nothing false or unworthy.

As My presence and My influence increase daily, not one element of striving. *Brush aside* the darkness and, with resolution, walk in My light boldly...

You are precious in My sight.

(Isaiah 43.4)

Evil always awaits an opportunity to bring you into sin. This can *not* affect My promises to you, as long as there is true sorrow and My forgiveness.

As you become increasingly victorious over ways of sin you have found that occasions of falling are now vividly experienced.

When *will* you trust Me? Evil's influence is petty compared with My power.

As you surrender yourself anew to Me (at *any* time - no matter what has gone before), there is a changed situation.

Continue to allow My influence (steadfastly refusing doubt) as I shield you.

**I have prayed for you,
that your faith will not fail you.**

(Luke 22.32)

As you deliberately choose to walk on that higher plane, in the light of My presence, know that evil is powerless to influence you. In every situation it must be instinctive to choose the light.

As you keep within the brightness of My love for you, you can trust Me, completely to keep evil at bay.

You know that you have a large measure of freedom – *the freedom of My love* – as long as you observe the principle of avoiding hurt to Me.

Yielding yourself to My influence every day, do not forget that a corresponding *wisdom is* yours, which you can follow courageously.

**Knowing these things,
you will be happy in carrying them out.**

(John 13.1 7)

I want you to make My *love* the driving-force behind each victory which you win.

Cultivate that firmness in following the way which I have shown you, without compromises. Remember the *effort* of choice – until it becomes second nature for you.

As soon as you recognise that you are following one of the old ways, turn to the light and embrace *Myself,* as the intruder is surrendered.

The *calling upon Me* – often helplessly – can always be made in utter trust in My coming to help you in your weakness.

Be strong, for I accompany you.
(Haggai 2.4)

$\mathcal{T}$here is always an attempt by evil to deceive you.

Yes, it *has* deceived you when it has prevented you from bringing every situation to My love; it has deceived you when forcing you to act in haste, or to doubt, temporarily, My power to uphold and protect you; it has deceived you when leading you into fear of consequences, even though sensing that a course was My will.

Remember that although you are aware of evil's activity you need *never* be subject to it. I want you to step out, resisting all evil's challenges; you can *observe* Me carrying you through to victory, as you defy those challenges.

**Satan has wished to have you,
in order to sift you like wheat.**

(Luke 22.31)

My light illuminating all that is in the present, robbing it of every jarring circumstance. As My light shines *in* you, there will be, unfailingly, My precious peace to meet needs. Always be aware of My understanding, so that you can *rest* upon it, letting it remove all other desire.

Bring to Me any circumstance as soon as it arises... so that My immediate influence can be upon it. Do not react stressfully, but simply hand the matter to Me – silently where you must.

My child, the work of *transforming* . . . making the circumstances which you give to Me work for your good, because of My affection for you. Therefore, in every situation - so many not of your making – just fly to Me.

How *can* I fail you?

My burden is light.

(Matthew 11.30)

As you look towards the future, resolve to be true to Me; true to yourself; sensitive to the needs of those whose lives may be linked with yours.

There are aspects of the days which I have in My hand for you that you cannot know. Here, it will be the simple following-out of My way. Just lay good foundations: your walk with Me, your *prayerful* contacts with others.

Your future is safety in My love, for ever . . . see everything which happens on earth in relation to this. A partial appreciation of that ultimate experience is each day granted to you. My most solemn promise is that you will come to be with Me where I am, in glory . . . even though by a thorny road.

Joy, *always* . . . because I will let nothing take you astray from Me.

My child, I bless you. Completely rest your spirit, now, in My love.

To be with Me where I am, and to see My glory.
(John 17.24)

The road you have thus far walked with Me *must* mean the presence of more love in your heart... but deeply desire *even more!*

Let only what is of love be in you now . . . drawing out your love, both for Me and for My other children.

My love, reflected in you, can achieve great things; love succeeds where the intellect fails, and it succeeds where force fails; let it dominate every aspect of your existence.

Love . . . in its purest and truest sense . . . will be something with which you are, already, partially acquainted, when you finally pass into My immediate presence.

Until that time, My child, gaze into the *brightness* of My tender love.

Let that brightness continue to disperse fear as you tread the way with Me.

So that your joy may be complete.

(John 15.24)

Until you come into the full realisation of My immediate presence, I give to you all that you need, in awareness of that presence, to carry you through this world's experience.

Because of the limitations of being in the flesh, you have had to learn to walk trustingly, without blinding revelations of Myself. What I do promise you is that if you wish to tread My way, you can always find that sense of My presence as stronger than present conditions.

Seeing your relationship with Me as the vital factor in your life, you cultivate a wise detachment about earth's variable fortunes.

My child, see this world as a unique training ground in which the spiritual increases all the time, preparing you for that for which you and I both long. Surrender all earthly anxieties as My love fills your consciousness.

Make sure that your treasure is in heaven.

(Matthew 6.20)

My children need to know how full of delight is the life spent in My presence, in the realm of the spirit. Everything not of harmony, everything not of love, and peace, will be swept away. It will be a life of self-forgetfulness, where only truth will shine.

In My presence, those who have struggled through the earthly existence faithfully, and kept alive the hope which I gave them, will build upon that which has been developed in them.

Already, those who have passed your way are, at My bidding, active in sharing My purposes of love. Love *is all* . . . the pure prompting of love and the rewards of love. All is designed to draw many more souls to the higher plane which I have prepared for them.

You, too, My child, can be sure of this great and unequalled vocation, as each day you thank Me... that you are Mine *forever* that you are My servant *forever.*

**I will give the fountain
of the water of life, freely.**

(Revelation 21 .6)

THE WAY FORWARD

I have given men the raw material of their inheritance. In their choices, and in their faithfulness to My way, the enrichment of their whole being by My promises is worked out. There is a promise-*creation* involved in that close walk with Me.

My child, in looking to Me for life's needs, the very look establishes promise-fulfilment. The sense of promise in your own heart becomes more sure. You see the future *filled* with Myself, and you experience the gradual exclusion of all that is not of Me.

My presence shines on all your experiences, and turns them into opportunities for consolidation of your inheritance.

See My promises as far above anything which could be devised by man. See them as an expression of love . . . an *eagerness* for you to enjoy what I am preparing for you.

If you are tempted to feel that a promise is merely a self-created hope, immediately gaze once more into the love-light of Him who watches over you. You will then see that I and My promises are *indivisible* . . . and your trust and expectancy can then return!

A state of true worship exists in that inter-play of your trust and My love. From yourself, I receive the assurance of your loyalty and continued walk with Me; from Me, you have the priceless sense of a love shown in My promised joy and provision.

You can now see why My servants were unaffected by the conditions of life in which they were placed because of their allegiance to Me. Upholding them was the immovable hope of realising My promises. Their fixed goal ensured their being *lifted up* into the love-promise sphere, where the hurts of this world are neutralised. You, too, My child, must resolutely tread this way . . . letting the world's experiences merely serve to strengthen the relationship with the Promise-Maker.

What you see as you look to Me is a hand outstretched . . . welcoming you to the realm of promise, reaching to bring you closer into that realm. This, more than all striving or planning, ensures your arrival at your true destination.

The *centrality* of Myself, and of the promise embodied in Me, will now draw together every potential of your life.

Banking upon the faithfulness of My promises means that in the foreground of your life, all the time, is My influence. A child-like trust in My word represents true spiritual maturity.

My child, promises which you cherish for yourself now make the decisive difference in your spirit-walk through a fallen world.

Your spirit is set free by My promises, and depends for its supply on all that I am, rather than on what the world can give!

* * * * * * * * *

NOTES

NOTES

NOTES

IN TIME OF NEED
or
IN LIFE'S CRISES

ANXIETY, FRETFULNESS
12, 55, 68, 83, 127, 154, 190, 195, 208, 210, 225

BEREAVEMENT
8, 26, 108, 132, 169, 241

FORGIVENESS
6, 64, 67, 93, 124, 159, 168, 174, 181, 193, 199, 220, 229

GUIDANCE
18, 69, 77, 90, 103, 148, 150, 195, 198, 207, 213, 228

LONELINESS, SPIRITUAL ISOLATION
5, 8, 14, 29, 33, 156, 171, 214, 229

RELATIONSHIPS, RECONCILIATION
44, 74, 92, 110, 117, 137, 164

SLEEP   12, 27, 78

SUDDEN CRISES
15, 22, 63, 83, 113, 135, 143

TIME OF DARKNESS AND UNCERTAINTY
8, 17, 26, 34, 46, 68, 78, 84, 102, 109, 113, 132, 135, 143, 169, 204

TIME OF DOUBT
5, 7, 97, 109, 121, 132, 173, 190, 192, 237, 241

GENERAL THEMES

COMMUNION WITH HIM
    21, 23, 38, 51, 52, 55, 76, 119, 154, 185

THE CROSS
    3, 67, 88, 91

DISAPPOINTMENTS, REVERSES
    30, 105, 111, 123, 133, 135, 212

DIVINE LONGING
    51, 221, 226

HIS FAITHFULNESS"
    28, 48, 56, 80, 121, 173, 180, 190

THE FUTURE
    122, 126-128, 139, 147, 162, 183, 212, 258–261, 263–5

THE INCARNATION
    2, 32, 59, 65, 134, 192, 218

GOD'S KINGDOM, HIS NEARNESS
    5, 13, 61, 97, 100, 128, 196, 218, 222

HIS LOVE IN CREATION
    2, 105, 140, 169

OBEYING HIS WORD
    24, 25, 37, 42, 50, 75, 85, 87, 99, 116, 131, 138,
    155, 158, 165, 187, 191, 207, 211, 228, 231

GENERAL THEMES

PRAISE AND WORSHIP
9, 51, 57, 84, 88, 151, 166, 217

PRAYER, INTERCESSION
53, 81, 92, 96, 110, 152, 164, 194

HIS PROMISES
130, 139, 162, 209, 234, 237, 242-244

HIS PROTECTION AND PROVISION
5, 36, 48, 68, 72, 78, 80, 97, 112, 113, 129, 149, 180, 182, 206, 227

RENEWAL
28, 46, 55, 76, 93, 102, 154, 177, 185, 193, 199, 219, 224

SANCTIFICATION
40, 49, 91, 94, 95, 104, 116, 136, 142, 144, 160, 161, 170, 172, 178, 179, 189, 209, 215

SERVING HIM
19, 43, 45, 62, 114, 118, 125, 139, 141, 145, 146, 175, 188, 189, 201, 230, 233

HIS SUFFICIENCY
54, 56, 80, 123, 149, 163, 174, 184, 186, 194

HIS SUPREMACY, HOPE OF MANKIND
1, 10, 16, 28, 71, 115, 122

Continued ......

GENERAL THEMES

TEMPTATION
    41, 58, 66, 90, 94, 120, 148, 153, 165, 167, 203, 213, 236

TRUST
    11, 39, 47, 54, 60, 82, 107, 121, 149, 152, 163, 176, 182, 210, 223, 232

UNITY WITH HIM
    4, 31, 35, 70, 73, 144, 170, 172, 178, 200, 205, 216

VICTORY IN HIS STRENGTH
    20, 41, 75, 79, 86, 89, 101, 106, 153, 157, 190, 194, 197, 206, 215, 220, 223, 235

* * * *

ADDITIONAL COPIES

If you wish to obtain copies of *I Am With You* for friends or others in need, they are available from the distributors below (in addition to the publishers, John Hunt Publishing Ltd. Tel: 01962 736880. Fax: 01962 736881).

Distributors:

- STL, PO Box 300, Carlisle, Cumbria CA3 0QS, UK. Tel: 0800 282728
- New Life: 60 Wickstead Avenue, Luton, Beds. LU4 9DP, UK. Tel: 01582 571010
- Bridge Books and Music, 14 North Bridge Street, Sunderland SR5 1B, UK. Tel: 0191 5673544

YOUNG PEOPLE'S EDITION

Especially for younger readers, Our Lord's words, given in time of prayer, are included in this special edition – in response to numerous requests.

Important teaching is given about God, His nature, His relationship with us, and about living successfully as a Christian.

Like the 'parent' book, this edition is in handsome hardcover – suitable for daily use over a long period; the book is available only from the distributors, **BRIDGE BOOKS AND MUSIC** or **NEW LIFE**.

* * *

Other titles by Father John include:

    The Friendship of Jesus

    God's Opportunities

    God's Promises

    Getting to Know Jesus *(for 9–10 year olds)*

    "Hello, Jesus!" *(for 7–8 year olds)*

    Fives and Sixes Meet Jesus

    Meet Jesus

and are available only from the distributors, **BRIDGE BOOKS AND MUSIC** or **NEW LIFE**.

* * *

"I AM WITH YOU" Cassettes

Selections from *I Am With You* have been recorded on cassette with the titles 'Friend', 'Trusting' and 'Achieving'. These three tapes make ideal listening for the daily quiet-times. Many have spoken of how these cassettes have a remarkable healing quality – including those who are incapacitated, or do not always find reading easy or convenient.

The cassettes have been produced by Anchor Recordings, a leading British sound organisation. To possess both the book and the tapes will always be spiritually rewarding! The tapes can be obtained from **BRIDGE BOOKS AND MUSIC** or **NEW LIFE**.

* * *

"I AM WITH YOU" in BRAILLE

The Royal National Institute for the Blind have produced a Braille edition in three volumes. Please contact the distributors, **BRIDGE BOOKS AND MUSIC** or **NEW LIFE**.

* * *

Other titles by John Woolley available from
BRIDGE BOOKS AND MUSIC or NEW LIFE

The Friendship of Jesus
God's Opportunities
God's Promises
God's Secret
Prayers for the Family
Sorrow into Joy
Words of Power

and books for children

Fives and Sixes Meet Jesus
Getting to Know Jesus (for 11–14 year olds)
Hello, Jesus! (for 7–10 year olds)
I Am With You (Young People's Edition)
Meet Jesus

THE "I AM WITH YOU" FELLOWSHIP

A Fellowship of those who treasure *I Am With You* has a rapidly-growing number of members, drawn from all Christian traditions, and extending to many countries.

Fr John writes personally to each new Fellowship Member. He prays for the Members of the Fellowship every day. Fellowship Members are always welcome to write to him about any particular need.

There is no charge or subscription. If you would like to be a Fellowship member, please write to:

Revd John Woolley,
C/o NEW LIFE,
60 Wickstead Ave, Luton LU4 9DP, U.K.

or C/o BRIDGE BOOKS AND MUSIC,
14 North Bridge St, Sunderland SR5 1AB, U.K.

I would like to join the "I Am With You" Fellowship.

Surname .... Revd / Mr / Mrs / Miss

Christian Name ....

Address ....

....

Post Code .... Telephone ....